MW00769778

The Modern Mountain Cookbook

THE MODERN MOUNTAIN COOKBOOK

A Plant-Based Celebration of Appalachia

Jan A. Brandenburg

Foreword by Beth Feagan

UNIVERSITY PRESS OF KENTUCKY

Copyright © 2025 by The University Press of Kentucky

Scholarly publisher for the Commonwealth, serving Bellarmine University, Berea College, Centre College of Kentucky, Eastern Kentucky University, The Filson Historical Society, Georgetown College, Kentucky Historical Society, Kentucky State University, Morehead State University, Murray State University, Northern Kentucky University, Spalding University, Transylvania University, University of Kentucky, University of Louisville, University of Pikeville, and Western Kentucky University.
All rights reserved.

Editorial and Sales Offices: The University Press of Kentucky
663 South Limestone Street, Lexington, Kentucky 40508-4008
www.kentuckypress.com

Appalachian Vegan logo and fruit and vegetable illustrations by Kendra Brandenburg. Vegetable wallpaper illustration © VasilkovS/Shutterstock.com. Skillet illustration © artKaisen/Shutterstock.com.

Cataloging-in-Publication data is available from the Library of Congress.

ISBN 978-1-9859-0176-6 (hardcover : alk. paper)
ISBN 978-1-9859-0179-7 (pdf)
ISBN 978-1-9859-0178-0 (epub)

This book is printed on acid-free paper meeting
the requirements of the American National Standard
for Permanence in Paper for Printed Library Materials.

Manufactured in the United States of America.

Member of the Association
of University Presses

To Jake and Cody, who taught me that life is an adventure

Contents

Foreword

When Jan bought the house across the street, we were excited to have a new neighbor. But we were also a bit apprehensive: What would she be like? Would she be kind or aloof? Cool or problematic? Imagine my joy when I found out that Jan was a vegan, and even better, she was writing a vegan cookbook! I've been vegan for several years now, and I'm married to a confirmed omnivore, so I'm always on the lookout for tasty vegan recipes to entice my meat-loving hubby. Now I had a vegan comrade in the neighborhood!

Jan settled in and made herself at home, immediately endearing herself to all her new neighbors by dropping off incredibly delicious vegan food: muffins, biscuits and gravy, chili and cornbread, vegetable soup, spinach artichoke dip. It seemed like every time we turned around, she was cooking up a fabulous dish and sharing it. One of our elderly neighbors was undergoing cancer treatment and had lost her appetite—nothing tasted good. But she loved Jan's food, especially her banana bread and cranberry bread. When another older couple had health issues, Jan regularly brought them meals—she always cooked a bit extra to share. She would bring me little boxes of cookies to pass along to bell hooks, Berea College's Distinguished Professor in Residence, who loved sweet treats and didn't get out much in her final years. Jan has a generous heart. She loves sharing good food that is healthy and delicious. She's a one-woman campaign to get people to eat more vegetables and love every bite. And boy, does she know how to host a party. Her table is always beautifully set, and her huge wooden counter is crammed with tasty dishes: appetizers, main dishes, sides, and desserts—all vegan and all incredible. There is always laughter, pleasant conversation, music, and the gift of fantastic food at her table.

This cookbook is like being invited into Jan's home. She shares funny stories, family anecdotes, and bits of Kentucky wisdom. It is a delightful read, and the recipes are unpretentious and accessible. This book is one more manifestation of Jan's mission to share her love of vegan food. Even the most dedicated meat lovers, like my husband, will want to try her easy, affordable, scrumptious recipes. I've wanted the recipes for many of these dishes for a long time. Her cornbread is the best I've ever had. Her beer cheese is unparalleled. Her baked spaghetti makes you want to grab another helping. Friends, this book is like having the keys to the kingdom. At last, we have Jan's secret recipes. Let the party start!

Beth Feagan, Berea College

Introduction

The idea for *The Modern Mountain Cookbook* was not a lightning bolt. It came to me slowly, over the course of years of spontaneous recipes, alterations, and "veganizations" jotted down on index cards and in journals. It grew from my love of the regional cuisine I grew up with and is the culmination of many cooking successes and failures. Among the latter, my first soybean casserole springs to mind—a recipe that nearly caused a family mutiny and is not included in this book. Yet the slow coalescing of this project seems fitting for the type of food you'll find here.

Appalachian cooks have been simmering their garden harvests for years. Out of necessity, they cooked, canned, dried, and stored foods that would sustain them through the unpredictable Kentucky winters. My maternal grandmother would not have known the term *vegan*, but she could conjure incredible meals from the simplest vegetable ingredients harvested as she walked the rows of her backyard garden.

My paternal grandmother believed vegetarianism was a cult and looked askance at any mention of my dietary transgression. I coached my young sons not to use the *V*-word at family gatherings to avoid unwanted interrogation. However, she taught me much about the independent spirit of the cook. She had complete confidence that my middle-school best friend and I—with a combined baking experience of zero—could solo our way through a frosted red velvet layer cake. She instilled the curiosity that guided me through years of cooking experimentation. She also encouraged me to assemble a rooster on canvas out of kernels of colored corn (a perplexing but popular fad of the 1970s). That was a mistake, but I don't ever recall her cautioning me to not make a mess. Instead, she urged me not to be afraid to try something new. That may be the best advice we can embrace, both inside and outside the kitchen.

Members of my family worked primarily in the school system in Pulaski County, but they were also weekend warriors of the food industry. They ran restaurants at both the Pulaski County livestock market and the tobacco warehouse, serving food only on sale days at those two businesses. These were inauspicious beginnings for a future vegan pharmacist.

I hung out in the kitchen as my grandmother made as many as a dozen pies before 10:00 a.m., and I helped her cart them to the restaurants. I washed dishes as my uncle grilled burgers and prepared the "plate lunch" of the day. Later, I waitressed every single Saturday. Even after leaving for pharmacy school, I was expected to drive from Lexington back to Somerset on Saturday mornings to serve up coffee, pie, and the weekly special to the taciturn farmers who counted on us to feed them through their twelve-hour days.

Midway through my first semester of pharmacy school, the empty stockyard building mysteriously burned down. My father called me early on a Saturday morning, as I was getting ready to leave for work, and broke the news. He also jokingly accused me and my siblings of some involvement in the blaze. My alibi was watertight, but I can't deny that some celebrating took place that evening.

I still drive by the site when I visit Somerset. My sister and I complained incessantly about our ruined date nights, complexions, and social lives. We criticized the more verbose and less expedient auctioneers who dragged sales into the evening hours, thereby cutting into our socializing. Like typical teenage girls, we lamented the smell of grease that permeated our hair and clothing. But it was a shared experience of laughing and complaining and working and feeding hungry people. My life may have veered in the opposite direction when it comes to food choices, but I still participate in these same activities.

My life can be traced through my love affair with cooking. My first Easy Bake Oven, with its tiny lightbulb, was an epiphany. I was thrilled with the miniature creations I single-handedly guided into existence. I was Barbie, only better, because I could cook.

By adolescence, I had moved on to omelets and meatloaves. I cooked for any and all visitors and relatives. They played Paul McCartney's "Cook of the House" in my honor. I felt like I was Edesisa, Roman goddess of food and feasting. I was armed with a spatula.

After pharmacy school, I brought my mortar and pestle home to grind herbs and seasonings. I discovered I loved growing a kitchen garden. I began to focus solely on the beauty of vegetables in 1995 and never looked back. The more I cooked and learned, the more reasons I found to continue the journey. I have been vegan since 2006.

My first kitchen was cramped and ill-equipped, but that didn't deter me from spending countless hours making recipes I found in *Southern Living* and *Country Living*. I sent my husband to work with his lunchbox full of lemon-cornmeal cookies and giant Irish pasties. This fueled some colorful ridicule from his construction crew, and on more than one occasion he was asked, "What the hell is that?" I achieved a small victory the day one of his coworkers asked why he always had homemade lunches while they had to eat "brought ons"—a term I was unfamiliar with, but it apparently means store-bought.

I have had many different kitchens since then, but they have all been the soul of my home. It's where I sit to think and create, where my children spent the most time with me when they were young, where friends and family gather still. I am the long-standing hostess in my family for everything from birthdays to holidays, and I didn't want that tradition to change because of my dietary choices. So I made every effort to dispel the illusion that veganism means embracing exotic and unfamiliar ingredients and set out to re-create the foods that say "home" to my loved ones. Twenty-five years later, I still host our Thanksgiving meal. I don't serve turkey, but there's an accommodation for that centerpiece and every other traditional food one would expect at a Kentucky holiday celebration. I can still make my grandmother's Italian cream cake.

It isn't easy to remain a steadfast vegan in an area where deer antlers rise from pickup beds, bumper stickers read "My heart belongs to a coon-hunter," and my restaurant dining options can be counted on one hand. However, small-town life is for me. The mountains outside my window signify home. So I continue to cook, pack my lunch, and share my food with anyone willing to let me demonstrate the deliciousness of plant-based living.

I didn't set out to write about health or veganism. I wanted to create a food landscape that represents Appalachian culture and the foods I grew up eating and still love, while also being true to my ethical and environmental beliefs. I hope you find plenty of inspiration for nutritious meals in these pages and enjoy *The Modern Mountain Cookbook*.

Vegan Kitchen Essentials

Vegan Kitchen Essentials

E very cook has certain tools, staples, and tricks of the trade that make work in the kitchen run more smoothly. As a camper, I can whip up a meal with some very rudimentary supplies, but when I'm at home I enjoy the luxury of a high-speed blender, a food processor, and even a bread machine to make a working woman's life easier. Why not?

Here, I list just a few tools and ingredients that will make your kitchen experience a pleasant one. Use these suggestions as a basic guideline. If you have a pan, a sharp knife (I'm a bit of a slacker in this area, running for the sharpener only when my samurai son joins me in the kitchen), a spoon, and a fork, you'll be able to execute most of the recipes in this book. The most important thing is to connect with your kitchen and remember why we cook. When our daily lives get too busy or chaotic, when we feel out of touch with nature, food, and one another, cooking and eating together ground us. Speaking personally, it is also how I choose to serve in the world. One of my greatest pleasures is simply being a quiet observer as people visit and share food around the table. The way I see it, no piece of kitchen gadgetry can improve on that.

Tools

Blender
I use my blender almost every day. My sons can attest to this, having been awakened for most of their lives by the sound of

smoothies being made. I prefer a Blendtec because of the lengthy warranty. The manufacturer has replaced my motor twice with nary a complaint. Many swear by the Vitamix as well. Creamy sauces in the plant-based world often involve cashews or other nuts, so be sure the blender you select can withstand frequent heavy-duty use.

Bread Machine

A couple of my recipes use a bread machine for mixing and rising. I love the convenience of this device because it frees me to do other kitchen activities and provides a cozy, draft-free environment for the rising step. However, I never bake anything in the bread machine. I like to shape my own loaves and let them brown in the oven.

Cast-Iron Skillet

A cast-iron skillet is the perfect tool for making crispy cornbread. It is important to season cast iron, so once you make your purchase, oil up the skillet and give it a few test runs (empty) in the oven at 325 degrees for 20 minutes at a time. I wash mine with mild dish soap and water after each use and then immediately dry it thoroughly and reapply oil. This is one tool you want to keep in prime working condition.

Food Processor

A food processor need not be an expensive piece of kitchen equipment. A basic, medium-bowl processor aids in the preparation of cheese balls and various doughs, and making fresh breadcrumbs is a breeze.

Oven Thermometer

It's always a good idea to know the exact temperature of your oven when baking, and I can attest that the readout on the oven could very well be a lie. Pop an oven thermometer on a rack and adjust the temperature accordingly.

Ricer

A ricer is a low-tech gadget that makes foolproof mashed potatoes. Ricing produces a smooth and creamy texture that cannot be duplicated using a mixer. I really do swear by this tool, and it doesn't even use electricity, so you could take it camping or add it to your doomsday prep list.

Zester or Microplane Grater

The addition of fresh citrus zest to breads, dressings, and sauces is a game changer. This small and inexpensive tool ensures that the fresh taste of lemons, limes, and oranges is at your fingertips to amp up the flavor of your food with little effort.

Ingredients

Aquafaba

When this magical ingredient was discovered, the plant-based world rejoiced. Suddenly the impossible became possible! Aquafaba is nothing more than the brine from a can of chickpeas (other beans have brine, but chickpeas work best). The starchy liquid serves as a great binder, but it can also be whipped into a foam to use for cakes and pies. Lofty meringue is no longer out of reach. I have added it to recipes for chocolate pie and Italian cream cake, but don't stop there in your exploration of other uses for this amazing substance.

Egg Replacer

Vegans have discovered numerous ways to mimic the binding power of the egg. Various egg replacers are included in this book, as different types work best in different recipes. If you are in a hurry, you can always use an equivalent volume of the product Just Egg. It is simple and reliable and can be poured directly from the bottle.

Kala Namak
This earthy South Asian black salt only recently made a splash in vegan cookery, but it was a cannonball. Due to trace amounts of sulfuric compounds, it adds a rich umami profile, similar in taste to egg yolks. This makes it ideal for tofu scramble, potato salad, and deviled potatoes.

Liquid Smoke
Appalachian cooking traditionally uses animal products to lend a smokiness to foods, but liquid smoke provides the same flavor. I start with ¼ to ½ teaspoon and adjust to taste from there.

Meat Substitutes
The meat substitute market has exploded in recent years, saving animal lives and appealing to more omnivores than ever before. I have tried many of these products, and of course I have my favorites. Gardein products are consistent in taste and quality, and No Evil, a small company based in Asheville, North Carolina, also makes some delicious products. Impossible ground beef is my preference for meatloaf and burgers, while Gimme Lean sausage is my go-to for gravy. That said, brands tend to come and go. Experiment to see which products you prefer, or substitute basic seitan or tofu in adaptable recipes for a more whole-foods approach. There are many detractors when it comes to the faux meat market, but I am not among them. The broader the appeal, the more vegan meals consumed, which means happy animals, happy planet, happy me.

Plant Milks
I employ a variety of plant milks, depending on the recipe. For cornbread, I use only unsweetened soy milk; for baked desserts, oat or almond milk works well. I always purchase unsweetened varieties to avoid any flavors that might not benefit the recipe.

Tamari

Tamari is another indispensable umami staple in plant-based cooking. It's a soy-based sauce pressed from the liquid drained from miso paste, with its own distinct flavor. It is less salty than traditional soy sauce and is generally gluten free, if that is your preference. Use tamari to add depth and saltiness to soups, stews, and marinades.

Tofu

I prefer the texture of extra-firm tofu. I like to freeze tofu, then thaw and drain it before using it in any recipe. Freezing enhances the texture and ensures that the tofu will hold up to any type of preparation and the addition of other ingredients and flavors.

Tomatoes

I adore all types of fresh summer tomatoes, but in my humble opinion, the fire-roasted San Marzano is ideal for cooking. I buy cans of San Marzanos to use in sauces and soups. The smoky flavor is incomparable.

No matter what tools or ingredients you have, nothing will enhance your cooking experience as much as connecting with your kitchen space. Although I can be a bit messy when I cook (according to some), I take pride in keeping my kitchen clean and always ready to prepare a meal. I also like to have fresh flowers, candles, a clean apron, and a glass of wine. It's truly the little things that make all the difference.

Breakfast and Brunch

Sorghum Spice Coffee Cake   17

French Toast   18

Banana Nut Mini Loaves   19

Brunch Casserole   20

Tofu Scramble   22

Home Fries   23

Griddle Pancakes   24

Banana Pecan Waffles   25

Hash Brown Casserole   25

Breakfast Hash   27

2

Breakfast and Brunch

The hearty Appalachian breakfast is iconic for a reason. Biscuits and gravy, pancakes, fried potatoes, cooked apples, and cheese grits are among the staples of our regional breakfast cuisine. My vegan recipes jump right into the starting lineup without missing a beat.

During my sons' earliest homeschooling days, we undertook a little adventure that we now lovingly refer to as the "retreat." Basically, fueled by the postmodern plague of an overwhelming sense of busyness, we withdrew from the common culture for two months. The boys' dad agreed to temporarily be the sole breadwinner and serve as our link to necessities such as groceries and sundries. We turned off the phone and the TV and planted ourselves on our home base of two and a half acres to see what would happen. How would we feel? What would we miss? How would our days unfold?

We announced this plan to friends and family prior to launch. Not surprisingly, the news elicited reactions from healthy skepticism to complete incredulity. From the outset, we made it clear that all were welcome to drop by for a visit (obviously, there was no chance we would be out), and we were happy to communicate by snail mail. We read, cooked, wrote, and rambled as far as our feet could take us. And perhaps due to human beings' curious nature, we had more visitors during that two-month period than at any other time before or since.

Sunday was the most popular day for visiting, so we always planned brunch. Tofu scramble, pancakes, soy sausage, fried potatoes, biscuits and gravy, and a giant fruit plate rounded out the menu. Even now, preparing a beautiful Sunday brunch to share with family and friends still captures the essence of that once-in-a-lifetime event. Try it. Get out your champagne flutes and pour a mimosa. Retreat for the day.

Sorghum Spice Coffee Cake

My paternal grandfather, Leonard, loved nothing better than some sorghum biscuits. In his house, sorghum could make an appearance at any meal, stored in what looked strangely like a paint can. He would take a giant pat of butter, pour the sorghum syrup over the top, mix it to a creamy consistency, and slather it on my grandmother Elva's delicious biscuits or cornbread. At the time, I wasn't anxious to try his sorghum soup, but as an adult, I totally get it. Sorghum's light, unique flavor makes it my favorite stand-in for honey. This cake comes together quickly and is perfect for brunch, a hostess or host gift, or coffee with a friend.

TOPPING

¼ cup unbleached all-purpose flour

¼ cup sugar

2 tablespoons vegan butter

CAKE

1 cup unsweetened soy milk

1 teaspoon apple cider vinegar

2 cups unbleached all-purpose flour

1 teaspoon baking soda

1 teaspoon cinnamon

½ teaspoon ginger

½ teaspoon allspice

¼ teaspoon nutmeg

¾ teaspoon sea salt

1 cup vegan butter at room temperature

1 cup sugar

½ cup sorghum syrup

½ cup unsweetened applesauce

2 tablespoons egg replacer powder

Preheat oven to 325 degrees. Butter and flour a springform baking pan and set aside. Mix the topping ingredients in a small bowl by rubbing them together with your fingertips until a coarse, crumbly mixture forms. Set the topping aside. To make the cake, stir the vinegar into the soy milk and set aside to thicken. In a medium bowl, whisk together flour, baking soda, cinnamon, ginger, allspice, nutmeg, and sea salt. Set aside. Using an electric mixer at medium speed, beat the vegan butter, sugar, and sorghum for 2–3 minutes, occasionally scraping the sides of the bowl, until smooth. Add the applesauce and egg replacer powder and beat 3–4 minutes, until light and fluffy. To this, alternately add the flour mixture and the thickened soy milk, beginning and ending with the flour mixture. Pour the batter into the prepared pan, sprinkle the topping evenly over the batter, and bake for 40 minutes, or until a toothpick inserted in the center comes out clean. Cool on a wire rack. Loosen the sides of the springform pan and slice the cake into wedges.

Serves 10.

French Toast

The recipe for French toast was reportedly brought to America by early English settlers, but its roots can be traced back to the Roman Empire. Certainly there is no argument about its tastiness, since we're still making it centuries later. And its popularity in Appalachia is no surprise, as it ranks high on the frugal scale— stale bread being a must. The earthy Himalayan salt, kala namak, augments the flavor of vegan egg, and a splash of bourbon provides a special Appalachian touch (plus, I just like bourbon). Be sure the bread is thick, and if it isn't stale, you may want to leave it out overnight to ensure it doesn't get soggy when dipped in the batter.

1 cup all-purpose flour
2 teaspoons baking powder
2 teaspoons cinnamon
½ teaspoon nutmeg
½ teaspoon sea salt
½ cup vegan egg replacer
    mixture

¾ teaspoon kala namak
1½ cups almond milk
2 teaspoons vanilla extract
2 tablespoons bourbon
3 tablespoons canola oil,
    divided
¼ cup brown sugar

| 8 slices thick bread | Vegan butter |
| Confectioners' sugar | Maple syrup |

In a small bowl, whisk together the flour, baking powder, cinnamon, nutmeg, and sea salt. Set aside. In a measuring cup, whisk together the vegan egg and kala namak. Place the eggy mixture in a blender with the almond milk, vanilla, bourbon, 2 tablespoons canola oil, and brown sugar and blend until smooth. Add the dry mixture and blend until smooth. Transfer to a shallow baking dish. In a large nonstick skillet, heat 1 tablespoon canola oil over medium heat. Place each piece of bread in the batter, turning to coat both sides evenly. Let any excess drip off, place the bread in the skillet, and cook approximately 3 minutes on each side, until golden brown and crispy. Sprinkle with confectioners' sugar and top with vegan butter and maple syrup.

Serves 4.

Banana Nut Mini Loaves

If there was a family in town that didn't make banana bread regularly, I didn't know them. Overripe bananas were never tossed out! During my marching band days, banana bread was the original snack, and no competitive event was complete without it. I started preparing this recipe as muffins, but I switched to mini loaves to spare my coworkers from the guilty internal debate about eating too many. Now they can say, "I only had one!" Use ripe bananas, and be sure to give the soy milk–vinegar mixture time to thicken.

1½ cups soy milk	¾ teaspoon sea salt
1 tablespoon apple cider vinegar	2½ teaspoons cinnamon, divided
2⅔ cups unbleached all-purpose flour	½ cup vegan butter, divided
1½ teaspoons baking powder	¾ cup sugar
½ teaspoon baking soda	¼ cup vegan sour cream
	2 teaspoons vanilla

2 large bananas, mashed   ⅛ cup demerara sugar
½ cup chopped pecans

Preheat oven to 350 degrees. Oil and flour one 6-count mini loaf pan and line the bottom of each section with a sliver of parchment paper. Combine the soy milk and vinegar in a measuring cup and set aside to thicken. In a mixing bowl, whisk together the flour, baking powder, baking soda, sea salt, and 2 teaspoons cinnamon. Set aside. In a separate bowl, beat ⅓ cup vegan butter and the sugar with an electric mixer until fluffy. Add the thickened soy milk, vegan sour cream, and vanilla and continue mixing until well combined. With a wooden spoon or spatula, combine the flour and liquid mixtures, stirring until just combined, then fold in the mashed banana. Divide the batter evenly among the 6 loaf sections. Melt the remaining vegan butter and toss with ½ teaspoon cinnamon, chopped pecans, and demerara sugar. Sprinkle the mixture evenly over the top of each loaf. Bake for 25–30 minutes, or until golden brown and a toothpick inserted in the center comes out clean. Cool on a wire rack before removing from the pan.

Serves 6.

Brunch Casserole

This recipe started small—a nod to the many breakfast casseroles we threw together in my college days—but it just kept growing. As I prepped my tofu scramble, I thought, hmm, some potatoes would be good here. Then came the soy sausage, followed by mushrooms and peppers, then a cheesy sauce to pull it all together and some parsley for fresh flavor. The next thing I knew, I had a signature casserole that helps folks appreciate what brunch days are all about: stretchy pants and naps. This is an excellent dish to prepare the day before. I keep it in the refrigerator overnight and pop it in the oven to bake while I drink coffee, snuggle with my puppy, and await that first bite.

1 12-ounce package extra-firm tofu, drained and crumbled

1 tablespoon nutritional yeast

3 tablespoons olive oil, divided

1 medium onion, diced

1 tablespoon minced garlic

½ cup diced green bell pepper

8 ounces white button mushrooms, sliced

8 ounces soy sausage, crumbled

1 10-ounce package frozen hash browns, thawed

½ teaspoon dried thyme

½ teaspoon dried rosemary

1 teaspoon kala namak

1 teaspoon freshly ground black pepper

2 tablespoons vegan egg mixed with ¾ cup very cold water

¼ cup chopped fresh parsley, plus additional for garnish

¾ cup Basic Vegan Cheese Sauce (see chapter 11)

Preheat oven to 350 degrees. Toss the tofu with the nutritional yeast and 1 tablespoon olive oil. Place on a baking sheet lined with parchment paper and bake for 20 minutes. Remove from the oven and set aside to cool. Heat 1 tablespoon olive oil in a skillet over medium heat and add the onion, garlic, bell pepper, and mushrooms. Cook 5–7 minutes, or until the onions become translucent. Remove the veggies from the skillet and set aside. Wipe the skillet clean and add the last tablespoon of olive oil. Cook the soy sausage over medium-high heat, using a fork to break up any large pieces until it looks uniform and is evenly browned. Pour the sausage into a large casserole dish and add the tofu and ¾ of the hash browns. Stir in the vegetables, thyme, rosemary, kala namak, black pepper, vegan egg blend, parsley, and vegan cheese sauce. Top with the remaining hash browns and bake for 45 minutes, or until the potatoes are brown and the casserole is hot and bubbly. Remove from the oven and allow to sit for 10 minutes. Garnish with parsley and serve.

Serves 8.

Tofu Scramble

When you utter the word *vegan* or *vegetarian* in an omnivorous crowd, sometimes you can see a pallid, tasteless block of tofu form in their collective thought bubble. This image couldn't be further from the truth. Tofu is a versatile, nutritious flavor vehicle that can serve as anything from a main course to a creamy dressing. I refuse to be tofu shamed, and I unabashedly serve this delicious tofu scramble to anyone who drops by for breakfast. One time my teenage son woke me in the wee hours of the morning to inquire if we could host the band Oceano for the night. I agreed. (Surely that made up for some of my spontaneous homeschool adventures gone awry, such as the time we drove an hour and a half to a nature preserve, where a Jesuit priest waxed eloquent about his composting toilet.) The band arrived at around 4:00 a.m., and guess what they had for breakfast. That's right. Tofu scramble with sawmill biscuits and gravy—eaten with gusto and followed by compliments to the chef. Be tofu proud!

1 14-ounce block extra-firm tofu

2 tablespoons olive oil, divided

¼ cup nutritional yeast

½ teaspoon turmeric

½ teaspoon garlic powder

½ teaspoon onion powder

1 teaspoon kala namak

½ teaspoon freshly ground black pepper

½ teaspoon sea salt

1 tablespoon minced garlic

1 small onion, finely chopped

1 red bell pepper, diced

½ cup sliced white button mushrooms

2 tablespoons chopped fresh parsley

Preheat oven to 350 degrees. Drain the tofu well, crumble it into a medium bowl, and toss with 1 tablespoon olive oil and the nutritional yeast. Bake on a baking sheet covered with parchment paper for 20 minutes. Remove from the oven. Whisk the turmeric, garlic powder, onion powder, kala namak, black pepper, and sea salt together, sprinkle over the warm tofu, and set aside.

Heat the remaining 1 tablespoon olive oil in a skillet over medium heat. Sauté the minced garlic and chopped onion for 3–5 minutes, being careful not to overbrown the garlic. Add the bell pepper and mushrooms and sauté for 3 minutes more. Add the tofu. Stir to combine all the ingredients, then use a spatula to press the tofu. Cover and cook for 5–7 minutes, until lightly browned on one side. Use the spatula to turn the tofu mixture over and brown the other side. Turn the tofu into a bowl and toss with parsley. Serve with sawmill gravy and biscuits, hash brown casserole, or some crispy toast and jam.

Serves 6.

Home Fries

What can I say about the simple but delicious fried potato? It's an Appalachian staple. I included home fries in the breakfast section, but they are just as likely to pop up on a plate with pinto beans and cornbread or green beans and cooked apples. I like to dice, parboil, and drain the potatoes before frying. This allows them to brown nicely without sticking to the skillet. Feel free to shake up the seasonings to best accompany whatever you're serving with the home fries.

3 cups peeled and diced potatoes	½ teaspoon garlic powder
	½ teaspoon onion powder
1 tablespoon sea salt	½ teaspoon freshly ground
2 tablespoons olive oil	black pepper

Cover the potatoes with water in a large saucepan and bring to a boil. Stir in the sea salt and allow the potatoes to boil rapidly for 5 minutes. Drain, place the potatoes back in the pan, and hold it over the heat for a few minutes to allow the extra moisture to evaporate. Heat the olive oil in a large skillet. Toss the potatoes with garlic powder, onion powder, and black pepper. Fry until golden brown. Add more sea salt to taste, and serve hot.

Serves 4.

Griddle Pancakes

If you're a cooking enthusiast, you tend to read cookbooks and recipes like fiction. If it's good, you can't wait to get to the next page. If it's really good, you can't wait to get to the kitchen. Every recipe I read, including my own, is usually accompanied by some uninvited narrative from the tiny vegan critic who sits on my shoulder. She generally has a lot of opinions about salt, vanilla, and most other ingredients, but she was remarkably quiet about this recipe I adapted from Isa Chandra Moskowitz's *Isa Does It*. I whip up these pancakes on my Camp Chef griddle, along with some soy sausage, at every opportunity. Isa, from my Appalachian spirit to your Brooklyn one, cheers! And if you ever find yourself in eastern Kentucky, the mimosas are on me.

1 cup soy milk
2 teaspoons apple cider
   vinegar
1½ cups unbleached all-
   purpose flour
3½ teaspoons baking powder
1 teaspoon salt

2 tablespoons sugar
¼ teaspoon cinnamon
½ cup vegan egg replacer
   mixture
3 tablespoons canola oil
1 teaspoon pure vanilla
   extract

Combine the soy milk and vinegar in a measuring cup and set aside to thicken. In a large bowl, sift together flour, baking powder, salt, sugar, and cinnamon. Make a well in the center of the dry ingredients. Pour the milk mixture into the well, along with the vegan egg, canola oil, and vanilla. Using a fork, stir until all the flour is combined and the batter is thick. Let the batter rest for 10 minutes and preheat a skillet or griddle over medium-low heat. Lightly oil the skillet and use a measuring cup to add ⅓ cup batter to the skillet for each pancake. Cook until the pancakes begin to bubble and brown around the edges. Flip the pancakes, adding more oil as needed, and cook for another 3 minutes, or until golden brown. Serve with vegan butter, fruit, and pure maple syrup.

Serves 2.

Banana Pecan Waffles

This simple recipe is basically a bowl of oatmeal disguised as a waffle, so it is both delicious and nutritious. It is how I got my children to eat oatmeal when they were growing up, and it was one of the first recipes my son wanted to make when he started to cook. You will be tempted to peek at the waffles as they cook, but be strong. Give them a full 10 minutes to develop their crispy exterior. Top with vegan butter, warm maple syrup, and additional pecans or fruit.

2 cups rolled oats	1 tablespoon sugar
1 tablespoon flax meal	1 teaspoon vanilla
2 cups water	½ teaspoon salt
1 banana	¼ cup pecans

Combine all the ingredients except the pecans in a blender and blend until smooth. Allow the batter to rest for 10 minutes to thicken. Pour half the batter onto a hot waffle iron sprayed with cooking oil. Sprinkle half the pecans over the waffle and cook for 10 minutes. Repeat with the remaining batter. Serve immediately.

Serves 2.

Hash Brown Casserole

During my college years in Lexington, there was a restaurant called TW Lee's that served an awesome Sunday brunch. Whenever the stars aligned—meaning I wasn't working and I wasn't broke—I loved to visit for the delicious hash brown casserole and spicy Bloody Marys. This is my vegan version of that favorite dish, which starts with cream of celery soup. Now I can enjoy it anytime, and so can you.

VEGAN CREAM OF CELERY SOUP

½ cup vegan butter

½ cup chopped onion

½ cup chopped celery

1 teaspoon minced garlic

2 bay leaves

½ teaspoon garlic powder

½ teaspoon onion powder

½ teaspoon celery seed

1 tablespoon dried parsley

¼ cup unbleached all-purpose flour

½ cup whole raw cashews

1 cup no-chicken broth

CASSEROLE

1 2-pound bag frozen hash browns, thawed

1 16-ounce container vegan sour cream

1 cup shredded vegan cheddar, divided

2 tablespoons chopped fresh parsley, divided

1 teaspoon sea salt

1 teaspoon freshly ground black pepper

½ cup cracker crumbs

Preheat oven to 350 degrees. Oil a 9- by 13-inch baking dish and set aside. To make the vegan cream of celery soup, melt the vegan butter in a medium saucepan and add the onion, celery, garlic, and bay leaves. Simmer on low heat for 10 minutes to allow the bay leaves to impart their flavor. Add the garlic powder, onion powder, celery seed, and parsley. Sprinkle the flour over the vegetable mixture. Cook and stir for 5 minutes. Remove from the heat and set aside. In a high-speed blender, process the cashews until they are finely ground. Add the broth and continue blending until the mixture is smooth and creamy. Remove the bay leaves, add the vegetable mixture to the blender, and process for 2 minutes, until the soup appears uniform and thick.

To make the casserole, combine the thawed hash browns with the soup mixture, vegan sour cream, ½ cup vegan cheddar, 1 tablespoon parsley, sea salt, and black pepper in a large bowl.

Stir well to combine, and spread evenly in the prepared baking dish. Top with the remaining cheddar and cracker crumbs. Bake covered with foil for 30 minutes. Remove the foil and bake another 15 minutes, until brown and bubbly. Top with the remaining fresh parsley and serve.

Serves 6–8.

Breakfast Hash

My maternal grandmother, Mae Moores, was both a great cook and an expert at stretching the food budget. This hash may have been her method of using up leftovers, but it was one of my favorite dishes. Served over toast or biscuits with lots of freshly ground pepper, it's both filling and delicious. Gravy plus potatoes? Sign me up. Don't wait until the day after Thanksgiving to make it.

3 tablespoons olive oil
½ cup chopped onion
2 cups diced faux turkey or chicken
1½ cups cubed cooked potato
3 tablespoons unbleached all-purpose flour
3 cups unsweetened oat or almond milk
1½ teaspoons vegan Worcestershire sauce
1 tablespoon chopped fresh parsley
1 teaspoon freshly ground black pepper
1 teaspoon sea salt

Heat the olive oil in a large skillet over medium heat. Add the onion and cook for 5 minutes, or until the onion starts to turn translucent. Add the faux meat and potato and cook until lightly browned. Sprinkle the flour over the mixture, stir until well coated, and cook until the flour begins to brown. Add the milk and stir until the mixture is thick and bubbly. Add the remaining ingredients and mix well. Adjust seasoning if needed. Serve over hot biscuits or toast.

Serves 4–6.

Sandwiches

Roasted Jalapeno Pimento Cheese Spread   32

Eggless Tofu Salad   32

Seitan Sandwich with Mashed Potatoes
and Mushroom Gravy   34

Fried Green Tomato Burger   34

Chick'n Salad Sandwich   36

The Best Spicy Fried Chick'n Sandwich   36

Tempeh Reuben   38

Sloppy Joes   39

"Catfish" Battered Tempeh Sandwich   40

Filet-o-Artichoke Sandwich   41

Tuna Melt Reimagined   42

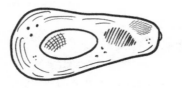

3

Sandwiches

When my kids were small, one of our favorite songs was "Sandwiches," by children's musician Fred Penner. He sang, "Sandwiches are beautiful, sandwiches are fine, I like sandwiches, I eat them all the time, I eat them for my breakfast and I eat them for my lunch, if I had a hundred sandwiches, I'd eat them all at once." We all agreed that Fred was a wise man. For vegans, it's easy to spread some peanut butter and jelly on bread, but other sandwich fare is more elusive and requires some vegan-savvy revamping. Due to my rural location, my life requires a lot of lunch packing. The jalapeno pimento cheese spread, eggless tofu salad, and chick'n salad recipes in this chapter are easy sandwich fillings that travel well for a work lunch or my favorite—the spontaneous picnic! I have also included options for hot sandwiches. The fried green tomato burger served with creamy slaw is especially satisfying if your mood calls for a hot sandwich as a quick dinner.

Roasted Jalapeno Pimento Cheese Spread

This spicy favorite is a good choice to accompany chili, spread on a veggie burger, or make small appetizer sandwiches or biscuits. The time it takes to slowly roast the peppers is worth it to achieve the smoky flavor profile. I like to buy vegan cheddar as a block and use a box grater for authenticity. You can adjust the cayenne up or down, depending on your heat tolerance.

1 large red bell pepper
1 jalapeno
2 7.5-ounce blocks vegan
    cheddar, grated
¾ cup vegan mayonnaise
1½ teaspoons vegan
    Worcestershire sauce

¼ teaspoon cayenne pepper
¼ teaspoon paprika
½ teaspoon sea salt
½ teaspoon freshly ground
    black pepper
Whole-grain bread, lettuce,
    and tomato

Turn the oven on broil. Place the jalapeno and bell pepper on a foil-lined baking sheet and roast until charred, checking and turning frequently. Place the peppers in a bowl and cover with plastic wrap. Cool for 15–20 minutes. When the peppers are cool, remove the skins and seeds. Dice the peppers and place them in a medium bowl along with the grated vegan cheddar. Whisk together the remaining ingredients and stir into the cheese and peppers until fully combined. Adjust seasonings and serve on whole-grain bread with lettuce and tomato.

Serves 6.

Eggless Tofu Salad

Where has kala namak been all my life? A relative newcomer to the American vegan game, kala namak, a kiln-fired Himalayan black rock salt, has been used for years in the savory regional dishes of India and Nepal. A darling of the ayurvedic world, it has a high sulfur content that makes it ideal for deepening the flavor of tofu. Add this tofu-based salad to a "cold plate," have it as an accompaniment to soup, or serve it on rolls for a perfect appetizer sandwich. The dash of Tabasco adds a nice touch, but feel free to omit it if you are entertaining a spice-sensitive crowd.

1 16-ounce block extra-firm tofu

1 tablespoon extra virgin olive oil

1 teaspoon kala namak

¼ teaspoon freshly ground black pepper

1 large celery stalk, finely chopped

1 large or 2 small shallots, finely chopped

1 tablespoon chopped flat-leaf parsley

1 large dill pickle, finely chopped

2 tablespoons chopped red bell pepper

½ cup vegan mayonnaise

1 tablespoon spicy Dijon mustard

½ teaspoon dried dill weed

½ teaspoon turmeric

1 tablespoon nutritional yeast

Salt and freshly ground black pepper to taste

Dash Tabasco

Preheat oven to 350 degrees. Line a baking sheet with parchment paper or no-stick aluminum foil. Drain the tofu and chop into a medium dice. In a medium bowl, toss together the olive oil, kala namak, and black pepper and add the diced tofu. Spread the tofu on the baking sheet and bake for 15 minutes. Remove from the oven and cool to room temperature. Place the cooled tofu in a bowl and add the celery, shallots, parsley, dill pickle, and bell pepper. Stir to combine. Whisk together the vegan mayo, Dijon, dill, turmeric, and nutritional yeast. Pour this mixture over the tofu and vegetables and mix well. Adjust salt and pepper to taste and chill for at least 1 hour before serving. Top with a dash of Tabasco.

Serves 6.

Seitan Sandwich with Mashed Potatoes and Mushroom Gravy

This is what I call Appalachian vegan diner fare. If that makes you want to grab a loaf of white bread to soak up all the extra gravy, I won't judge. These sandwiches are an especially good choice for those nonvegans who fret that they'll leave the table with growling bellies and a beard full of alfalfa sprouts. Prepackaged seitan is available at most grocery stores. In keeping with the diner spirit while sneaking in some cruciferous nutrition, I like to serve this hot sandwich with creamy coleslaw (see chapter 5).

2 8-ounce packages traditionally seasoned seitan, thinly sliced

2 tablespoons extra virgin olive oil

1 teaspoon vegan Worcestershire sauce

1 recipe Mushroom Gravy (see chapter 11)

1 recipe Creamy Mashed Potatoes (see chapter 9)

2 slices bread

Prepare the mashed potatoes and gravy. In a skillet over medium heat, cook and stir the seitan and olive oil for 4–6 minutes, until the seitan is slightly brown but not crunchy. Remove from the heat. Toss with the vegan Worcestershire sauce. Pour the seitan into the gravy and stir to combine. To serve, cut 2 slices of bread into triangles and arrange half on a plate with mashed potatoes in the center. Spoon a layer of the gravy mixture over the bread, top with the remaining slices, then add more gravy to the top of the bread and mashed potatoes.

Serves 6.

Fried Green Tomato Burger

Fried green tomatoes are a southern favorite. In my very small hometown of Irvine, Kentucky, Michael's was a popular restaurant that served up a homestyle buffet that drew people from

miles around. It was the landmark that put Irvine on the map
for a lot of folks. My diet made it especially hard to order lunch
from Michael's, until I hit on the idea of substituting a fried green
tomato for my burger. The first time I called in this order, the
restaurant called me right back, assuming they had misunder-
stood. After I placed the order several times, the staff got curious and gave it a try themselves. Maybe I was on to something.
Pickling the green tomatoes prior to frying gives this sandwich
extra zing.

2 large green tomatoes, cut
    into 1½-inch slices
½ cup water
½ cup plus 1 teaspoon apple
    cider vinegar, divided
1 tablespoon sugar
½ teaspoon salt
½ cup soy milk
1 tablespoon vegan egg mixed
    with ½ cup very cold water

1 teaspoon hot sauce
1 cup cornmeal
1 tablespoon Creole seasoning
Canola oil for frying
Sea salt and freshly ground
    black pepper to taste
Buns, lettuce, tomato, and
    coleslaw

In a medium saucepan, bring the water and ½ cup vinegar to
a boil. Add the sugar and salt to the boiling water and stir to
dissolve. Add the tomato slices and boil for 2 minutes. Remove
from the heat, cover, and let stand for 15 minutes. Drain and pat
the slices dry. Mix the soy milk with 1 teaspoon vinegar and set
aside to thicken for 15 minutes before stirring in the vegan egg and
hot sauce. Whisk together the cornmeal and Creole seasoning
and pour into a shallow dish. Heat ¼ inch of canola oil in a large
skillet over medium-high heat. Dip the tomatoes in the soy milk,
then dredge in the cornmeal mixture and sprinkle with sea salt
and black pepper. Fry the slices in the heated skillet until golden
brown, about 4–6 minutes on each side, reducing the heat if necessary. Adjust the seasoning. Serve 1–2 tomato slices on heated
buns with lettuce, tomato, and coleslaw.

Serves 4.

Chick'n Salad Sandwich

If you like your salad with pecans and grapes, by all means, toss these healthful additions into the mix. My family would greet this deviation with a baleful eye, so I stick to the basics. This salad is quick to prepare and keeps for several days if covered and refrigerated, making packing lunch a breeze.

2 cups chopped vegan chick'n
½ cup diced celery
1 tablespoon finely chopped
    fresh parsley
2 tablespoons finely chopped
    red onion
¾ cup vegan mayonnaise
2 tablespoons dill relish

1 tablespoon lemon juice
½ teaspoon kala namak
1 teaspoon freshly ground
    black pepper
½ teaspoon sea salt
Whole-grain bread, lettuce,
    and tomato

Preheat oven to 350 degrees. Place the vegan chick'n pieces on a foil-lined baking sheet and bake for 15 minutes. Set aside to cool. Meanwhile, combine the remaining ingredients in a medium bowl and mix well. Taste and adjust the seasoning and add more lemon juice if needed. Serve on toasted whole-grain bread with lettuce, tomato, and additional vegan mayo.

Serves 6.

The Best Spicy Fried Chick'n Sandwich

I adapted this recipe from a *Bon Appetit* article I read several years ago. It's a pretty long list of ingredients, but did you really want the second-best spicy fried chick'n sandwich? I didn't think so.

6 frozen vegan chick'n patties
    (not breaded)
4 teaspoons sea salt
2 teaspoons brown sugar

2 teaspoons baking powder
1½ cups unbleached all-
    purpose flour
⅓ cup cornstarch

1 tablespoon garlic powder

1 tablespoon onion powder

1 tablespoon paprika

2 teaspoons cayenne

1 teaspoon poultry seasoning

2 tablespoons sea salt

1 cup soy milk

1 tablespoon apple cider vinegar

2 tablespoons bourbon (optional but recommended)

1 tablespoon vegan egg mixed in ½ cup very cold water

3 tablespoons hot sauce

¾ cup vegan mayonnaise

1 teaspoon chopped garlic

1 tablespoon dill pickle brine

2 tablespoons chopped fresh chives

½ teaspoon celery seed

½ teaspoon sea salt

½ teaspoon freshly ground black pepper

Peanut oil for frying

Buns, vegan butter, lettuce, tomato, and vegan mayo

In a small bowl, mix the sea salt, brown sugar, and baking powder. Rub the frozen chick'n patties with the mixture and place back in the freezer. Whisk together the flour, cornstarch, garlic powder, onion powder, paprika, cayenne, poultry seasoning, and sea salt and pour into a shallow dish. Add the vinegar to the soy milk and set aside to thicken for 15 minutes. Add the bourbon, vegan egg, and hot sauce to the thickened soy milk and whisk thoroughly. Combine the vegan mayo, garlic, pickle brine, chives, celery seed, salt, and pepper and mix well. Refrigerate the mayo mixture until ready to use. Dip the frozen patties in the soy milk mixture, then roll in the flour mixture. Allow the patties to sit for 5 minutes, then repeat this step, pressing the batter into the patties to ensure adherence. Heat the peanut oil over medium-high heat. When the oil is hot, place the patties in the skillet and cook until golden brown, 5–7 minutes on each side, lowering the heat if necessary. Serve on grilled buttered buns with lettuce, tomato, and mayo.

Serves 6.

Tempeh Reuben

Vegan Swiss cheese is harder to find than other vegan cheeses, so if it proves to be elusive, you can substitute provolone, jack, or cheddar. I use a traditional Russian dressing because the zippy taste of horseradish complements the other flavors. However, Thousand Island dressing also works, and a bottled vegan product is available if you're short on time.

1 8-ounce package smoked tempeh bacon, halved and sliced into thin strips

1 tablespoon extra virgin olive oil

½ cup vegetable broth

2 teaspoons vegan Worcestershire sauce, divided

½ teaspoon onion powder

½ teaspoon garlic powder

1 tablespoon tamari

1 cup vegan mayonnaise

1 tablespoon very finely chopped red onion

¼ cup chili sauce

1 tablespoon horseradish

1 teaspoon hot sauce

¼ teaspoon paprika

½ teaspoon sea salt

4 slices vegan Swiss cheese

½ cup sauerkraut, drained

8 slices vegan rye or marble rye bread

Heat the olive oil in a small skillet over medium heat. Add the sliced tempeh and brown for 2 minutes. Combine the broth, 1 teaspoon Worcestershire sauce, onion powder, garlic powder, and tamari in a measuring cup and pour over the tempeh. Simmer for 10 minutes, allowing most of the liquid to evaporate, then remove from heat. To make the dressing, stir together the vegan mayo, red onion, chili sauce, horseradish, hot sauce, paprika, and sea salt in a small bowl. Place the bread slices on a baking sheet with cheese and tempeh on half the slices and sauerkraut on the other half. Heat under the broiler, watching closely, until the cheese begins to melt. Pour the dressing on the kraut side, put the two halves together, and slice in half. Serve with brined cucumbers and chips.

Serves 4.

Sloppy Joes

Easy-peasy dinner sandwiches are our friends. You could open a can of sloppy joe sauce, but why not step up your sandwich game with this simple one-dish wonder? Invite the veggie skeptics over, whip up some slaw and oven-fried potatoes, and break out a bag of Oreos for dessert. You will have a fan club of small children and other picky eaters holding out their plates.

1 12-ounce package vegan ground crumbles	1 teaspoon cumin
3 tablespoons extra virgin olive oil, divided	¾ teaspoon sea salt
	2 tablespoons sorghum syrup
1 small onion, chopped	1 teaspoon vegan Worcestershire sauce
1 large stalk celery, chopped	
2 teaspoons chopped garlic	1 tablespoon country Dijon mustard
1 green bell pepper, chopped	
1 8-ounce can tomato sauce	2 tablespoons red wine vinegar
1 cup water	
¼ cup tomato paste	Salt and freshly ground black pepper
½ teaspoon dried oregano	Whole-grain buns

Heat 1 tablespoon olive oil in a large nonstick skillet over medium-high heat. Lower the heat to medium and brown the ground crumbles for 7–10 minutes, stirring frequently. Remove from the skillet and set aside. Wipe any residue from the skillet before adding the remaining 2 tablespoons olive oil. Heat the oil over medium heat and then add the onion, celery, garlic, and bell pepper. Sauté for 10 minutes, or until the vegetables are soft, being careful not to overbrown the garlic. While the vegetables are sautéing, place the remaining ingredients in a small bowl and whisk to combine. Stir the sauce into the vegetable mixture, add the crumbles, and simmer for 30 minutes. Remove from the heat and allow to sit for 10 minutes before serving on whole-grain buns.

Serves 6.

"Catfish" Battered Tempeh Sandwich

This recipe takes a little planning. The tempeh has to be simmered and then soaked overnight in a kelp bath to give it a more authentic "catfish" flavor. Tempeh is high in protein and vitamins, and it contains prebiotics to keep our bellies happy. Toast a bun and mix up some vegan tartar sauce (see chapter 11) to add some creamy goodness to this sandwich. Alternatively, you can slice the tempeh into nugget shapes and serve it as a main course.

1 package tempeh, sliced in half and then sliced lengthwise into 4 squares
½ cup vegetable broth
1½ cups soy milk
1½ tablespoons apple cider vinegar
2 tablespoons plus 2 teaspoons kelp granules, divided
1 teaspoon hot sauce

1 cup cornmeal
½ teaspoon unbleached all-purpose flour
1 teaspoon sea salt
½ teaspoon cayenne
1 teaspoon garlic powder
1 teaspoon freshly ground black pepper
1 teaspoon Seafood Magic (a blend of herbs and spices)
Canola oil for frying

Place the sliced tempeh and vegetable broth in a medium skillet over medium-high heat and turn to coat the tempeh. Adjust the heat to a simmer and cook for 10 minutes, turning the tempeh occasionally. Mix the soy milk and vinegar and set aside to thicken. Add 2 tablespoons kelp and the hot sauce to the milk mixture. Place the cooled tempeh in a shallow dish and pour the milk mixture over the top, ensuring that the tempeh is submerged. Cover and refrigerate 8 hours or overnight.

Whisk together the remaining 2 teaspoons kelp granules, cornmeal, flour, sea salt, cayenne, garlic powder, black pepper, and Seafood Magic and pour into a shallow dish. Remove the tempeh from the kelp soak and roll each slice in the cornmeal batter, coating all sides evenly. Pour ½ inch of canola oil into a large skillet and heat to medium-high. Fry the tempeh slices in the hot oil for 6–7 minutes on each side, or until golden brown.

Serves 4.

Filet-o-Artichoke Sandwich

Sea vegetables, such as kelp, are rising stars in the cooking world due to their powerful umami flavor. Their glutamate content provides a flavor boost much like soy sauce or Worcestershire sauce, and they contain natural iodine and B vitamins, including B12. This patty makes a tasty sandwich, but it can also be served bunless with a side of rice and vegetables.

3 tablespoons extra virgin olive oil
1 medium onion, chopped
1 stalk celery, chopped
1 14-ounce can hearts of palm, drained, patted dry, and chopped
1 6-ounce jar artichoke hearts, drained, patted dry, and chopped
½ teaspoon onion powder
½ teaspoon garlic powder
2 teaspoons Seafood Magic

1 tablespoon cornstarch
1 teaspoon kelp
¼ cup vegan mayonnaise
¼ cup whole wheat breadcrumbs
½ cup cornmeal
½ cup unbleached all-purpose flour
Canola oil for frying
Buns, Tartar Sauce (see chapter 11), lettuce, and tomato

Heat the olive oil in a skillet over medium heat. Add the onion and celery and sauté for 10 minutes, or until the onion is translucent. Place the hearts of palm and artichoke hearts in a medium bowl. Add the sautéed vegetables and the onion powder, garlic powder, Seafood Magic, cornstarch, kelp, mayo, and breadcrumbs to the bowl and mix well. Shape the mixture into 6 equal-sized patties. Whisk together the cornmeal and all-purpose flour and roll the patties in the mixture, pressing the cornmeal-flour blend into the patties to ensure they are well coated. Cover and chill for 30 minutes. Wipe the skillet clean, cover the bottom with approximately ¼ inch canola oil, and heat over medium-high heat. Place the chilled patties in the skillet and cook for 10 minutes on each side, or until evenly browned. Serve on toasted buns with tartar sauce, lettuce, and tomato.

Serves 4.

Tuna Melt Reimagined

This star-studded vegan version of a tuna sandwich is a longtime favorite that is chock-full of vegetables, protein, and flavor. To take it to the next level, this recipe re-creates the classic tuna melt. There are several brands of spicy vegan cheeses to choose from.

1 15-ounce can chickpeas, rinsed, drained, and roughly mashed with a potato masher

¼ small red onion, finely chopped

1 large carrot, finely chopped

1 large stalk celery, finely chopped

¼ cup sunflower seeds

2 tablespoons sweet relish

1 tablespoon whole-grain mustard

1 tablespoon dulse flakes

1 teaspoon kala namak

1 tablespoon fresh lemon juice

1 teaspoon dried dill

2 tablespoons chopped fresh parsley

⅓ cup vegan mayonnaise

Hot sauce to taste (I use a couple of dashes)

Salt and freshly ground black pepper to taste

Toasted whole-grain bread, vegan mayo, spicy vegan cheese slices, lettuce, and tomato

Stir all the salad ingredients together in a medium mixing bowl until well combined. Chill until ready to use. To prepare the melts, heat oven to 425 degrees. For each sandwich, spread one slice of toasted bread with vegan mayo and the salad mixture and top with a slice of vegan cheese. Place on a baking sheet and bake just until the cheese is melted, 3–4 minutes. Top with lettuce, tomato, and the remaining toast slices. Serve with pickles and chips.

Serves 6.

Appetizers and Snacks

4

Appetizers and Snacks

In the 1990 movie *Mermaids*, Cher plays a mom whose entire cooking repertoire is built around a book about appetizers. The guy from *Who Framed Roger Rabbit* gets all squirrely about food on sticks and people perching on countertops to eat and suggests having a "normal" family dinner. However, I understand the appeal of this unorthodox dining ritual. Appetizers and small plates are fun! They let us sample a variety of foods without going overboard, and they can stand alone when we're not in the mood for something heavy. On days when I work late, preparing some fried green tomatoes or a simple bean dip with chips might be the extent of my cooking ambition. When I have family and friends over, I like to have several options for snacking as people arrive. I want to accommodate a variety of taste preferences and give everyone some time to catch up, grab a beverage, and relax. Some of the simple dips presented here are quick to prepare, and others can be made well in advance. I love the spinach artichoke dip, and a tasty vegan cheese ball is just the thing for holiday gatherings. However, as a Kentuckian, it goes without saying that beer cheese is a regular feature on my appetizer menu. After all, we invented it.

Spicy Bean Dip

This is one of my favorite ways to be thrifty and use up leftover beans. If you don't have leftovers, canned pinto or black beans work just as well. When I take an afternoon walk past my former coworker Andrea's new place of employment, she often yells out, "I need bean dip!" Here it is, Andrea. I usually top this dip with scallions and vegan cheese or sour cream and serve it with tortilla chips, but it can also be used for street tacos or bean and vegan cheese quesadillas.

2 cups cooked pinto or black
    beans, rinsed and drained
½ red onion, coarsely
    chopped
1 tablespoon minced garlic
1 cup fresh tomatoes, seeded
    and coarsely chopped
1 jalapeno, seeded and diced

2 tablespoons hot sauce
1 teaspoon cumin
2 tablespoons chopped fresh
    cilantro
Garnish: 2 tablespoons
    chopped scallions and
    vegan sour cream

Combine all the ingredients (except the garnish) in a food processor and pulse on high speed until smooth. Pour into a serving dish and garnish with chopped scallions and vegan sour cream, if desired. Serve with additional hot sauce and tortilla chips.

Serves 6.

Soy Sausage Cheddar Balls

These festive and flavorful bites enhance the old standby by adding cayenne, onion, and fresh parsley. I made these for my last employee party, and my son, who is always drafted into helping me at these gatherings, got to eat only two (and he really likes them). Turns out, my coworkers think vegan sausage balls are just fine. The maple mustard dipping sauce is like icing on the cake.

SOY SAUSAGE CHEDDAR BALLS

1 cup unbleached all-purpose
    flour
½ teaspoon sea salt
¼ teaspoon freshly ground
    black pepper
½ teaspoon cayenne
1½ teaspoons baking powder
1 8-ounce package shredded
    vegan cheddar or
    cheddar-jack

1 14-ounce package bulk soy
    sausage
1 small onion, finely chopped
3 tablespoons vegan butter,
    melted
2 tablespoons finely chopped
    fresh flat-leaf parsley

MAPLE MUSTARD SAUCE

½ cup vegan mayonnaise
¼ cup country Dijon mustard

3 tablespoons pure maple
    syrup

Preheat oven to 400 degrees. Line a large baking sheet with
parchment paper. To make the balls, whisk together the flour,
sea salt, black pepper, cayenne, and baking powder in a large
bowl until well combined. Add the vegan cheese, tossing to coat
with flour. Add the sausage, onion, vegan butter, and parsley. Use
your hands to work the ingredients together until the mixture is
uniform. Shape into 40–45 1-inch balls. Place the sausage balls on
the baking sheet, ½ inch apart. Bake 25 minutes, or until golden
brown. To make the dipping sauce, whisk together the vegan
mayo, Dijon, and maple syrup and keep it chilled until ready to
serve. Serve the sausage balls warm with the dipping sauce.

Serves 10–12.

Spicy Beer Cheese

We take the art of making beer cheese seriously in Kentucky. Just across the river from my home county of Estill, the town of Winchester holds an annual festival dedicated to this favorite appetizer and party snack. Beer cheese originated in Winchester in the 1940s at a place known as Johnny Allman's, but it has since achieved nationwide popularity, with good reason. It's delicious! Beer cheese always tops the list of my game-day snacks (Go Cats!). I serve it with crispy crackers, celery, carrots, and radishes. This adaptation was inspired by a recipe from Maggie Green's *The Kentucky Fresh Cookbook*. It has plenty of heat, so feel free to dial down the cayenne if you prefer a milder version. I like to use Tick Licker, a crisp and hoppy India pale ale (IPA) from the nearby Dreaming Creek Brewery in Richmond, Kentucky, for its great flavor (and admittedly because Tick Licker is fun to say). I allow it to sit overnight at room temperature to go flat. Be sure to verify that the brew you choose is vegan. Some brewers use animal products in the clarification process, but there are plenty of vegan options available.

1 7-ounce block vegan cheddar, cut into a medium dice
8 ounces vegan cream cheese
1 tablespoon minced garlic
1 tablespoon hot sauce (I use the Kentucky-based

Screamin' Mimi's Pepper Sauce)
1 teaspoon vegan Worcestershire sauce
½ cup flat IPA
¼ teaspoon cayenne

Allow the cheese to come to room temperature. Place all the ingredients in a food processor or high-speed blender (the soup speed works well) and process until completely smooth. Pour into a container, cover with plastic wrap, and press the wrap onto the top of the mixture. Refrigerate overnight or for several hours prior to serving.

Serves 8–10.

Fried Green Tomatoes

Fried green tomatoes rank high on my list of favorites. I've included them in the appetizer chapter, but there's no reason not to serve them as a side dish. Just omit the garnish and roll out the skillet corn, green beans, mashed potatoes, and cornbread. They also make a great sandwich topped with vegan cheese, slaw, and red onion on a toasted bun, or they can take the place of a burger (see chapter 3). You will not be disappointed.

4 large green tomatoes, cut into thick slices and salted
1½ cups soy milk
1 tablespoon apple cider vinegar
1 teaspoon kala namak
1 teaspoon Tabasco
2 cups cornmeal
2 tablespoons Creole seasoning

½ teaspoon sea salt
½ teaspoon freshly ground black pepper
¼ cup olive oil
Sea salt and freshly ground black pepper to taste
Garnish: vegan sour cream, chopped cilantro, and additional Tabasco

Mix the vinegar with the soy milk and set aside to thicken. Add the kala namak and Tabasco and whisk. In a shallow dish or pie plate, sift together the cornmeal, Creole seasoning, sea salt, and black pepper. Dredge each tomato slice in the cornmeal mixture and let it sit for 5 minutes. Dip the tomato slices in the soy milk; then redredge in the cornmeal mixture. Refrigerate for 10 minutes. Meanwhile, heat the olive oil in a nonstick skillet over medium heat and preheat the oven to 300 degrees. Remove the tomatoes from the refrigerator in batches as you fry them. Cook 3–4 minutes on each side, or until golden brown. Place the fried tomatoes in the oven on a baking sheet lined with parchment paper to keep them warm. When all the tomatoes have been fried, add sea salt and black pepper to taste. Garnish with vegan sour cream, chopped cilantro, and additional Tabasco if desired.

Serves 4–6.

Party-Time Cheese Ball

I recently added this party favorite to my entertaining menu, and I think it's a keeper. I now realize that mining some of those 1970s party clichés may be in order. I do love a good theme party, especially if I know all the music. Put on your leisure suit, break out the Chex Mix, and stir up a party drink with a sparkly swizzle stick! And if you're feeling especially retro inspired, keep in mind that those little cellophane packages of Club Crackers that adorned every 1970s party tray are vegan.

1 cup chopped pecans, divided

1 8-ounce container vegan cream cheese at room temperature

1 7-ounce block vegan cheddar, finely grated

1 tablespoon country Dijon mustard

1 tablespoon vegan mayonnaise

1 teaspoon vegan Worcestershire sauce

1 tablespoon vegan butter, melted

2 tablespoons dry white wine

¼ cup finely chopped scallions

½ teaspoon freshly ground black pepper

¼ cup finely chopped flat-leaf parsley

Toast all the pecans in a skillet over medium heat for 5–10 minutes, or until fragrant. Cream together the vegan cream cheese and cheddar with an electric mixer. Add the Dijon, vegan mayo, Worcestershire sauce, melted butter, wine, scallions, black pepper, and ¼ cup pecans. Continue mixing until all the ingredients are thoroughly incorporated. Shape the mixture into a ball and wrap in plastic wrap. Chill for 1–2 hours. Remove from the refrigerator and shape into 2 balls. Roll each ball in the remaining chopped pecans and fresh parsley to coat the outside. Rewrap and chill until ready to use. Serve with crackers and raw vegetable dippers.

Serves 8–10.

Cucumber Dill Dip

My best friend's mom always gave us 7-Up and Pringles when we had belly aches—a magic cure for any ailment when you're twelve. I'm pretty sure I feigned an illness or two during those years. As our health improved—usually a rapid process—we were allowed to add a delicious and cooling cucumber dill dip. This is my version of Martha's healing fare. If you're serving it as a party appetizer rather than a cure-all for woeful adolescents, some bourbon goes great with the 7-Up.

1 medium cucumber, peeled, seeded, and finely grated
½ cup vegan sour cream
½ cup vegan cream cheese, softened
1 tablespoon dried dill

1 tablespoon dried minced onion
2 teaspoons fresh minced garlic
1 tablespoon fresh lemon juice
¾ teaspoon sea salt

Combine all the ingredients in a food processor and process until completely smooth. Cover and chill for at least 2 hours prior to serving. Serve with mixed raw vegetable dippers and crackers or chips.

Serves 6–8.

Fried Mushrooms with Horseradish Dipping Sauce

Irvine, Kentucky, is home to the Mountain Mushroom Festival, where we celebrate the morel, the uncontested queen of the mushroom family. In actuality, the morel is more akin to a truffle than a mushroom, and its unmatched earthy flavor can be addicting. This is complicated by the fact that morels are relatively rare, and those folks who hit the woods on warm, wet spring mornings to collect them are not likely to divulge their favorite hunting grounds. If morels are not available, use any other mushroom of your choice. Add the quick-to-make dipping sauce for a perfect appetizer any time of year.

MUSHROOMS

8 ounces mushrooms, rinsed
  and dried

1 cup flour

2 teaspoons salt

1 teaspoon black pepper

1 teaspoon garlic powder

1 teaspoon onion powder

1 teaspoon apple cider vinegar

½ cup soy milk

1 tablespoon vegan egg mixed
  with ½ cup very cold water

1 cup cornmeal

½ cup canola oil

DIPPING SAUCE

¼ cup vegan mayonnaise

¼ cup vegan sour cream

1 tablespoon fresh lemon juice

2 tablespoons white wine
  vinegar

2 tablespoons vegan prepared
  horseradish

¼ teaspoon salt

⅛ teaspoon cayenne

Prepare the dipping sauce by stirring together all the ingredients until completely incorporated. Place in the refrigerator to chill.

For the mushrooms, mix the soy milk and vinegar and set aside to thicken. Sift together the flour, salt, black pepper, garlic powder, and onion powder and place in a shallow dish or pie plate. Roll each mushroom in the flour mixture, turning to coat all sides. Set aside. Add the vegan egg to the soy milk mixture and whisk. Place the cornmeal in a shallow dish or pie plate. Heat the oil in a skillet over medium-high heat. Dip each mushroom in the egg mixture and dredge in the cornmeal. Allow to sit for 5 minutes; then fry for 5 minutes on each side, or until the coating is crispy and brown. Serve warm with the dipping sauce.

Serves 2–4.

Onion Dip

This is a great all-purpose dip for entertaining or when you want to plop down in front of your current Hulu binge with a bag of kettle chips. No judgment here. Before I became vegan, dips were an easy option to grab from the grocery store shelf on movie night or to whip up at home by stirring a soup packet into some sour cream. A vegan lifestyle can whittle down the prepackaged options, but no worries. This tasty vegan version of the classic onion dip is quick to make. We need not sacrifice our snacking traditions.

½ cup vegan sour cream
½ cup vegan mayonnaise
¼ cup vegan cream cheese
2 tablespoons dried minced
    onion
½ teaspoon garlic powder

½ teaspoon sea salt
¼ teaspoon freshly ground
    black pepper
1 tablespoon dried parsley
1 tablespoon dried chives

Combine all the ingredients and beat with an electric mixer until smooth. Chill for at least 2 hours prior to serving. Serve with your choice of chips and raw vegetable dippers.

Serves 6.

Stuffed Mushroom Caps

My mother married my stepfather, Danny, on Valentine's Day. That was very romantic, but it also meant they would be celebrating their doubly special day along with the entire world. After years of their frustrating attempts to dine out on the busiest day for the restaurant industry, we came up with a solution: I would make them dinner in-house. The youngest grandsons would be my waitstaff, and in keeping with the double theme, the live entertainment as well. Dressed in tiny suits with white towels draped over their arms, they took the diners' orders (albeit a limited menu), wobbled the food to the table, played semirecognizable versions of songs on the fiddle and mandolin, and recited poetry.

These mushrooms were Danny's favorite vegan dish, so they were always the appetizer. Every year, he shared one or two with my mom and then ate the rest. He washed them down with a side of Elizabeth Barrett Browning and the boys' squeaky version of "Cotton-Eyed Joe" that literally brought a tear to your eye. This recipe is delicious and deceptively easy, and it doesn't require a special occasion or musical accompaniment to warrant its addition to the menu. You can prepare the mushrooms ahead and pop them in the oven a few minutes before serving.

1 pound fresh white mushrooms	1 tablespoon finely chopped flat-leaf parsley
2 tablespoons olive oil	½ teaspoon sea salt
2 tablespoons minced shallot	¼ teaspoon freshly ground black pepper
1 teaspoon minced garlic	
½ cup whole-grain breadcrumbs	¼ teaspoon paprika
	¼ cup vegan parmesan

Preheat oven to 400 degrees. Remove the stems from the mushroom caps and finely chop the stems. Heat the olive oil over medium heat. Add the mushroom stems, shallot, and garlic and sauté for 5 minutes. Stir in the breadcrumbs, parsley, salt, pepper, and paprika and heat for 2 minutes. Taste the mixture for seasoning and adjust if necessary. Stuff each mushroom cap with the mixture, place in a nonstick baking pan, and top with the vegan parmesan. Bake for 15–20 minutes, or until the caps are tender.

Serves 6.

Spinach Artichoke Dip

This rich dip is my appetizer Achilles' heel. The creamy, flavorful cashew base is well worth the extra effort required to make it. I almost always serve this dip at large gatherings, but I have to curb my overenthusiasm during the taste-testing process. I pop the dip in my mini crock to keep it warm until ready to serve with tortilla chips. If you're lucky enough to have leftovers, this dip will keep in the fridge for 2 days. Just reheat and serve.

2 tablespoons vegan butter
2 15-ounce cans artichoke
    hearts packed in water
2 shallots, minced
2 tablespoons minced garlic
½ cup white cooking wine or
    other dry white wine
½ cup cooking sherry
½ cup cashews
½ cup water
1 cup no-chicken broth
½ cup nutritional yeast flakes

2 teaspoons dried thyme
½ teaspoon crushed red
    pepper flakes
1 tablespoon fresh parsley
6 cups baby spinach, sliced
    into thin ribbons
1 teaspoon sea salt
½ teaspoon freshly ground
    black pepper
Smoked paprika (for garnish)
¼ cup shredded vegan
    parmesan (optional)

Melt the vegan butter over medium heat and add the artichokes, shallots, and garlic. Cook, stirring frequently, for 6–8 minutes, or until the vegetables begin to soften. Add the wine and sherry and cook for another 1–2 minutes to allow the alcohol to evaporate. Place the cashews, water, and broth in a high-speed blender and process until completely smooth. Stir the nut mixture into the vegetables along with the nutritional yeast, thyme, and red pepper flakes. Cook, stirring occasionally, for 40 minutes. Stir in the fresh parsley. Add the spinach a handful at a time and cook for another 10 minutes, or until the spinach is softened. Stir in the sea salt and black pepper. Pour into a serving dish or crock and garnish with smoked paprika and vegan parmesan. Serve warm with tortilla chips, crackers, or pita wedges.

Serves 6.

Fruit Plate with Dip

Since the under-ten set may react to savory appetizers like they're lined up to receive their flu shots, I've included this fruity option complete with a sweet and tangy dip that will please kids of all ages. I arrange the fruit in an aesthetically pleasing pattern, making it worth their time to dig in and destroy it. And if they happen to be around during prep time, the kids can easily help with that. While I can't guarantee an Instagram-worthy outcome, it's the perfect opportunity to reinforce that "it's the process, not the product."

2 cups fresh pineapple chunks

2 cups fresh cantaloupe cubes

2 cups grapes

2 cups strawberries, washed and hulled

2 cups kiwi slices

8 ounces vanilla Greek-style vegan yogurt

½ cup vegan cream cheese, softened

1 tablespoon pure vanilla extract

4 tablespoons pure maple syrup

Zest of 1 lemon

Arrange the fruit in the artful pattern of your choice. Combine the yogurt, cream cheese, vanilla, maple syrup, and lemon zest and whip with an electric mixer at medium speed until creamy and smooth. Chill the fruit and dip until ready to serve.

Serves 8–10.

Potato Cakes

Potato cakes are how we Appalachians use up leftover mashed potatoes. But oddly, this is not how I became a fan of the humble latke. At age eighteen, while on an admirably spontaneous but poorly planned trip to Key West during Christmas break, I wound up broke in Miami's Little Havana. You know your trip has gone off the rails when you have to drive twelve hours from your initial destination to find a place to sleep. Right around the corner from my shabby residence, which by all appearances doubled as the hotel boiler room, was a place called Hilda's. Hilda served up potato cakes from morning to evening. They were hot, crispy, filling, and, most important, cheap. I came back to Kentucky with a special fondness for the food that kept me going for that week in Florida. I like to serve these with either vegan sour cream and fresh parsley or applesauce.

2 cups mashed potatoes

2 tablespoons fresh minced onion

2 tablespoons finely chopped fresh parsley, divided

1 tablespoon vegan egg mixed with ½ cup very cold water, divided

½ teaspoon sea salt

¾ teaspoon freshly ground black pepper

½ cup unbleached all-purpose flour

1 cup fresh breadcrumbs

½ cup canola oil

Applesauce or vegan sour cream (optional)

Preheat oven to 300 degrees and place a parchment-lined baking sheet inside to heat. Combine the potatoes, minced onion, 1 tablespoon parsley, half the egg mixture, salt, and pepper and mix until fully combined. Shape the potato mixture into 8 balls. Cover and chill for 20 minutes. Dredge each ball in the flour and shake off any excess, then dip in the remaining vegan egg mixture and roll in the breadcrumbs. Press down slightly to form each ball into a disc. Set aside on a sheet of wax paper. Heat the oil in a nonstick skillet over medium-high heat. Add the potato cakes to the skillet 4 at a time and cook until golden brown, about 4 minutes on each side. Reduce the heat if they brown too quickly. Keep them warm in the oven until all the potato cakes are cooked. Serve immediately either plain or with your choice of toppings.

Serves 4.

Salads

5

Salads

Confession: I really, really love salad. I love green salad, pasta salad, fruit salad, and bean salad. However, before you condemn me for perpetuating the stereotype of the forlorn vegan munching on a raw carrot, know that this was a fact of my life long before I was vegan. I loved salad even before there was ranch dressing. I have been known to enter a restaurant intending to order hot fudge cake and, spying a salad bar of leafy greens, have a complete change of heart.

When I was in fifth grade, we briefly lived at a Holiday Inn in Durham, North Carolina, during a parental job transition. Temporarily without a kitchen, we ate most of our meals at the hotel dining room, with all expenses covered by the corporate expense account. One day, after rising early and feeling a bit peckish, I headed down to the restaurant to dine alone (without permission). I ordered a green salad with blue cheese dressing—for breakfast. The amused staff served my breakfast salad without comment. Unfortunately, there were repercussions for my lack of parental supervision and for playing fast and loose with the corporate expense account. But it was worth it.

I like my salads with crisp, cold, colorful ingredients, a handful of fresh herbs, and the zing of a homemade dressing. When we're contemplating dining out, I've been known to ask, "But do they have a good salad?" Clearly, I posed this question much more than I realized when my sons were growing up because they now parrot it back to me every time we try to reach a consensus on restaurant selection.

Salads are the yin to the yang of comfort food. If I start the day with a hearty breakfast casserole, chances are I'll want something light later. Salads are a good source of both nutrition and weight control for people like me who are always thinking about their next meal. Statistics show that losing as little as ten pounds can make a difference in blood pressure, and consuming foods at their freshest naturally reduces sodium consumption. Win-win, right?

Salads are the ideal medium for substituting ingredients. You can use your favorite vegetables, what's in season, or whatever you happen to have on hand to create the perfect salad. I have included basic side salads as well as other dishes that can make a light meal if you filled up on biscuits and gravy earlier in the day. As a wise Appalachian vegan yogi (me) once said, "Balance in all things." Okay, I didn't say it first, but it's true!

Favorite Tossed Salad

I like to include a large colorful tossed salad when making dinner for a crowd. It's simple yet much appreciated by guests. I think part of the enjoyment of salad consumption is the fact that some-one else went to the trouble of washing and chopping the compo-nents to create a rainbow of colors in a bowl. I admit I frequently farm this task out to willing volunteers so that I can experience the same pleasure. Whether tossed with a flavorful vinaigrette or topped with the ever-popular ranch dressing, a tossed salad is in the weekly rotation at my house. Be sure to thoroughly wash the ingredients. If you don't own a salad spinner, wash the romaine and place it in a clean cloth in the refrigerator to drain while you prepare the rest of the salad.

1 head romaine, chopped
1 cup small broccoli florets
1 cup small cauliflower florets
½ cup chopped carrots
1 medium cucumber, sliced
    longways into 6 sections
    and seeded and diced
1 cup chopped kale

¼ cup chopped flat-leaf
    parsley
1 yellow bell pepper, seeded
    and diced
1 tomato, diced and salted to
    taste
¼ cup toasted pumpkin seeds

Combine all the ingredients except the tomato and pumpkin seeds. Chill until ready to serve. Sprinkle the tomato and pump-kin seeds on top of the salad right before serving.

Serves 8.

Farmer's Market Corn Salad

I love the months when fresh corn is piled high in the produce markets. Kelly's Market in Richmond, Kentucky, has been one of the stops on my shopping rounds for decades, dating back to its days operating out of an awesome painted bus. Kelly's selections always include Silver Queen and Peaches and Cream, two of my

favorite corn varieties. This corn salad is one of my most frequently requested recipes. If your former spouse's new wife asks
you for the recipe, it must be good. At the peak of the Kentucky
growing season, this can be a beautiful and flavorful side dish or
a perfect topping for black bean cakes or tacos. The combination
of white balsamic vinegar and jalapeno complements the sweet
taste of freshly picked corn.

8 ears corn—kernels removed
    from the cob
3 tablespoons olive oil,
    divided
6 fresh tomatoes, chopped
2 cucumbers, seeded and
    chopped
1 green bell pepper, seeded
    and chopped
1 jalapeno, seeded and
    chopped
¼ cup chopped cilantro
4 tablespoons white balsamic
    vinegar
Salt and pepper to taste

Turn the oven to broil. In a casserole dish, combine the corn
with 1 tablespoon olive oil and toss until evenly coated. Place the
casserole dish under the broiler, checking and stirring frequently.
Remove from the oven when the corn starts to lightly brown.
Set aside to cool. Once the corn has reached room temperature,
add the rest of the vegetable ingredients and the cilantro. Whisk
together the remaining 2 tablespoons olive oil and the balsamic
vinegar and stir into the salad. Season with salt and pepper to
taste. Serve immediately or store in the refrigerator until ready
to use.

Serves 8.

Creamy Tangy Coleslaw

In Kentucky, slaw isn't just a side dish; it's a condiment. We pile
it on top of burgers, hot dogs, and barbecue sandwiches just as
happily as we serve it alongside fried tempeh and hush puppies.
The Wigwam restaurant in my hometown of Irvine, Kentucky,
is famous for its Country Boy, a double burger piled high with

slaw and fixin's. Variations of this cruciferous staple abound, but I think this one is the perfect blend of creaminess, zing, and crunch. My late stepmom and cook extraordinaire, Jo Sears, suggested the addition of Jane's Crazy Mixed Up Salt. I like a mixture of green and red cabbage, shredded carrots, and kale as the base, but any combination will work.

DRESSING

1 cup vegan mayonnaise
1 tablespoon white vinegar
1 tablespoon fresh lemon juice
1 tablespoon sugar
1 tablespoon Dijon mustard
1 tablespoon horseradish

1 teaspoon Jane's Crazy Mixed Up Salt
¼ teaspoon paprika
½ teaspoon celery seed
½ teaspoon black pepper

SLAW

1 red bell pepper, seeded and diced

8 cups slaw mix
Sea salt to taste

Whisk together the dressing ingredients. Combine the slaw mix with the bell pepper. Twenty minutes before serving, add the dressing to the slaw mix and chill. Salt to taste before serving.

Serves 8.

Cucumber Onion Relish

I know there's an artisanal pickle craze going on right now, but this relish has been served with dinner as far back as I can remember. It can be prepared any time of year, but it's a summertime favorite because everyone grows cucumbers, and it pairs perfectly with other fresh vegetables. Try it along with some green beans, new potatoes, and cornbread or on top of grilled veggie dogs. It's a quick and easy way to include some raw vegetables and healthy apple cider vinegar in your diet. The addition of the spicy jalapeno and Cholula is compliments of my son Jake.

2 cucumbers, seeded and diced	½ cup apple cider vinegar
1 medium sweet onion, diced	½ cup water
1 jalapeno, seeded and diced	1 teaspoon Cholula Hot Sauce
1 tablespoon chopped fresh parsley	1 teaspoon sea salt
	¼ teaspoon freshly ground black pepper

Combine all the ingredients and chill for 1 hour before serving. Serve with a slotted spoon to drain excess liquid.

Serves 8.

Picnic Potato Salad

This is a traditional southern potato salad just like my grand-mothers used to make (minus the eggs). All of our summer family gatherings and potlucks required potato salad—and lots of it. I boil the potatoes in salty water with the skins on, allow them to cool, and then peel and dice. Kala namak, a Himalayan black salt, imparts an eggy taste due to its high sulfur content. If you can't find it, use an equal amount of sea salt. As always, I like plenty of color and a variety of textures, hence the addition of red bell pepper, scallions, and fresh parsley. This potato salad pairs well with traditional fried chick'n, my vegan take on Nashville hot chick'n (if you like spicy), or barbecue seitan sandwiches.

3 pounds whole russet potatoes	1 cup celery, thinly sliced on the bias
1 tablespoon salt for the cooking water	⅛ cup finely chopped flat-leaf parsley
1 red bell pepper, seeded and diced	3 scallions, finely chopped— both white and green parts
	¼ cup sweet pickle relish

1 teaspoon kala namak
¾ teaspoon freshly ground
   black pepper
½ cup vegan mayonnaise
½ cup vegan sour cream

1 tablespoon yellow mustard
1 tablespoon apple cider
   vinegar
Salt and pepper to taste

Place washed potatoes in a large pot, cover with cold water, and bring to a boil. Add 1 tablespoon salt to the boiling water and cook uncovered for 20–25 minutes, or until potatoes are barely tender when pierced with a fork. Drain the potatoes and cool to room temperature. Peel and dice the potatoes and place in a large bowl. Add the red bell pepper, celery, parsley, scallions, relish, kala namak, and black pepper and stir gently to combine. Whisk together the vegan mayo, vegan sour cream, mustard, and vinegar and stir into the potato mixture. Add salt and pepper to taste. Chill until ready to serve.

Serves 6–8.

Pasta Salad

Almost everyone loves pasta salad. You can count on this recipe for a reliable picnic addition or any social occasion that requires you to satisfy the tastes of many with a single dish. Topped with some grilled vegan chick'n and parmesan, it makes a tasty light lunch or dinner. My favorite pasta for both salads and soups is ditalini. If it's not available, bowtie or rotini pasta works just as well.

16 ounces uncooked pasta
1 tablespoon sea salt for the
   cooking water
1 cup broccoli florets
½ cup chopped carrots
½ cup thinly sliced celery
1 red bell pepper, seeded and
   diced

1 cup cauliflower florets
1 small cucumber, seeded and
   diced
1 can small black olives,
   rinsed and drained
¼ cup chopped flat-leaf
   parsley
2 scallions, chopped

2 cloves garlic, minced
1 teaspoon fresh lemon zest
Red Wine Dijon Vinaigrette
  (see chapter 11)

Salt and freshly ground black
  pepper to taste

Add sea salt to boiling water and prepare the pasta according to package directions. Pour into a colander, rinse with cold water, and drain. Transfer the pasta to a large bowl. Add the remaining ingredients, stir in the desired amount of vinaigrette, and taste for seasoning, adding salt and pepper as needed. Chill until ready to serve.

Serves 8–10.

Macaroni Salad

This salad reminds me of the old roadside country stores that were prevalent when I was growing up. You could stop in at these family-owned and -operated establishments and get a sandwich, a soda, and often some macaroni or potato salad prepared by the family matriarch. Sadly, most of these places are no longer in business. My friend, who was enjoying a "recreational" road trip, found this out the hard way when she stopped at one of the old markets in need of sustenance, swung open the door with the Rainbow Bread sign, and found herself not at the market (which was long defunct) but in the middle of Mom and Pop's living room. They were shocked to have *Wheel of Fortune* so rudely interrupted, and she was extremely disappointed. A tomato sandwich, some macaroni salad, and a cold Mountain Dew would have hit the spot.

8 ounces elbow macaroni
1 tablespoon salt for the
  cooking water
2 large red radishes, grated
2 large carrots, grated
½ cup chopped celery

¼ cup chopped flat-leaf
  parsley
¾ cup vegan mayonnaise
¼ cup white vinegar
1 tablespoon sugar

½ teaspoon freshly ground
   black pepper

Sea salt and freshly ground
   black pepper to taste

Prepare the pasta according to package directions, adding salt to the boiling pasta water. Drain and rinse the pasta under cold water and transfer to a large bowl. Add the radishes, carrots, celery, and parsley and stir gently. Combine the vegan mayo, vinegar, sugar, and black pepper and whisk until completely blended. Pour over the pasta mixture and stir gently to coat the pasta and vegetables. Cover and refrigerate until ready to serve. Adjust the seasoning, adding salt and pepper if needed, just before serving.

Serves 8–10.

Strawberry Cucumber Salad

I always anxiously await the first crop of fresh local strawberries. These tiny powerhouses of flavor make the overgrown supermarket brands pale in comparison. This salad is as beautiful to look at as it is to eat, and it makes an excellent presentation when you want your table to look extra colorful. The flavor combination and the crunchy pistachios are an unexpected but delicious blend. So once you've had your fill of strawberry shortcake, give this salad a try.

4 cups (about 1 pound)
   strawberries, quartered
3 baby cucumbers, sliced
3 teaspoons sugar, divided
½ teaspoon ground
   cardamom

⅛ teaspoon sea salt
½ cup vegan sour cream
1 teaspoon fresh lemon juice
¼ cup roasted unsalted
   pistachios
⅛ teaspoon cayenne

Toss the strawberries and cucumbers with 1 teaspoon sugar, cardamom, and sea salt and set aside to allow the sugar to dissolve. Mix the vegan sour cream, 2 teaspoons sugar, and lemon juice in a small bowl and set aside. Pulse the pistachios and cayenne in a food processor until the nuts are finely ground (but be careful not to overprocess and wind up with nut butter). Divide the salad among 4 plates, drizzle the sour cream dressing over each plate, and sprinkle with pistachios.

Serves 4.

Tomato Peach Salad

This salad is a vibrant and flavorful union of fruits, vegetables, and herbs. I love to visit Kelly's Fruit Market in the summer and stock up on their delicious peaches, both for this dish and for a traditional peach crisp topped with vanilla cashew-milk ice cream. You can make the dressing a day ahead. Toss together the vegetables, herbs, and peaches right before serving along with some crusty bread or cheddar biscuits.

8 ounces vegan sour cream

4 tablespoons sherry vinegar, divided

4 tablespoons olive oil, divided

2 tablespoons tamari, divided

¼ teaspoon sea salt

3 medium ripe tomatoes, sliced into wedges

1 pint yellow cherry tomatoes, halved

2 medium peaches, sliced into wedges

½ small red onion, thinly sliced

1 large ear corn—kernels removed

2 tablespoons chopped fresh basil

2 tablespoons chopped fresh parsley

Sea salt and freshly ground black pepper to taste

To make the dressing, whisk together the vegan sour cream, 2 tablespoons vinegar, 1 tablespoon olive oil, 1 tablespoon tamari, and sea salt. Chill until ready to use. To make the salad, whisk the remaining 2 tablespoons vinegar, 3 tablespoons olive oil, and 1 tablespoon tamari in a large bowl. Add tomatoes, cherry tomatoes, peaches, red onion, corn, basil, and parsley to the bowl and toss to combine. Add salt and pepper to taste. Drizzle the dressing on chilled plates and top with the vegetable mixture. Garnish with additional herbs if desired.

Serves 4–6.

Kale and Brussels Sprouts Salad

This little gem is packed with nutrition and flavor. While working on my second yoga teacher certification, a fellow student brought this salad for everyone to share. It looked amazing! Unfortunately for me, it contained both honey and parmesan, which are not vegan-friendly. Judy was kind enough to share the recipe so that I could veganize it. I consider myself an experienced practitioner (if not a downright expert) in the realm of kale salads, and this one hits all the right flavor notes. It's substantial enough to be a full lunch all on its own. The onions can be pickled a day or two ahead as a time saver.

PICKLED ONION

1 large red onion, thinly sliced
3 tablespoons apple cider
    vinegar

2 teaspoons sorghum syrup
¼ teaspoon sea salt

DRESSING

1 tablespoon minced shallots
2 tablespoons Dijon mustard
¼ cup fresh lemon juice
1½ teaspoons fresh lemon zest

2 teaspoons sorghum syrup
¼ cup olive oil
Sea salt and freshly ground
    black pepper to taste

SALAD

1 bunch Lacinato kale, spiny
    stems removed and leaves
    chopped
1 small bunch curly kale, spiny
    stems removed and leaves
    chopped

1 pound brussels sprouts,
    trimmed and finely grated
1 cup toasted almonds,
    coarsely chopped
½ cup grated vegan parmesan

To make the pickled onion, bring a kettle of water to a boil. Place the red onion in a colander in the sink, pour the boiling water over it, and shake to drain. In a medium bowl, combine the vinegar, sorghum, and salt and mix well. Add this mixture to the onion and stir to coat. Pour into a mason jar, cover, and refrigerate for at least an hour or up to a couple of days. Shake occasionally to ensure that all the onion is exposed to the pickling liquid. To make the dressing, combine all the ingredients and set aside. To make the salad, toss together the kale, brussels sprouts, pickled onions, toasted almonds, and vegan parmesan in a large bowl. Add the desired amount of dressing and toss again to coat and combine. Serve immediately.

Serves 8.

Spinach Salad with Mushrooms and Red Onions

This salad is a good choice when neither tossed salad nor slaw seems just right. I often serve it on holidays when something fresh and green with a little bit of bite is needed to offset the other rich foods and beverages. It comes together quickly and can be assembled earlier in the day and then tossed with dressing right before serving. The pumpkin seeds add both nutrition and texture. If I'm serving this salad for lunch or as the sole accompaniment to a pasta or other one-dish main course, I increase the amount of pumpkin seeds to ¼ cup or substitute pecans or walnuts.

8 ounces baby spinach, stems
   removed
½ red onion, thinly sliced
8 ounces white button
   mushrooms, thinly sliced
¾ cup vegan mayonnaise
¼ cup red wine vinegar

1 tablespoon sugar
1 glove garlic, crushed
½ teaspoon Dijon mustard
Sea salt and freshly ground
   black pepper to taste
2 tablespoons toasted
   pumpkin seeds

Combine spinach, red onion, and mushrooms in a large bowl. In a small bowl, whisk vegan mayo, vinegar, sugar, garlic, and mustard until well blended. Toss with the spinach mixture immediately before serving. Season to taste with salt and freshly ground pepper. Top with toasted pumpkin seeds.

Serves 8.

Save-the-Tuna Salad

My dad wasn't much of a fisherman, so he wasn't offended when I tossed his infrequent catches back into Lake Cumberland as soon as they hit the bucket. I continue to protect the fish by serving this tasty salad. I have never lived close to the ocean, but I'm no stranger to blue water. I'm an avid follower of David Attenborough and know enough about the butterfly effect to realize that my choices, even in the heart of the mountains, can have a far-reaching impact on our planet's oceans and climate. In cooler seasons, I like to have this salad on a sandwich alongside some creamy tomato soup. In the summer, I add it to what we call a cold plate, which is basically a salad trio (take your pick), some raw fruits and veggies, vegan ranch dip, and crunchy whole-grain crackers on the side. It's also an excellent picnic choice. Canned chickpeas (garbanzo beans) are available everywhere. Save the bean brine to make some aquafaba meringue to top a pie or banana pudding.

2 14-ounce cans chickpeas,
   drained and rinsed

¼ cup chopped red onion
½ cup diced celery

¼ cup chopped dill pickle
¼ teaspoon minced garlic
2 tablespoons dried nori
   seaweed flakes

1 cup vegan mayonnaise
Sea salt and freshly ground
   black pepper to taste

Place the chickpeas in a large bowl and mash with a potato masher, but be careful not to end up with a puree. You want the chickpeas to retain some texture. Add the red onion, celery, dill pickle, and garlic. Sprinkle the seaweed flakes over the mixture and stir to thoroughly combine. Fold in the vegan mayo, making sure to coat all the ingredients. Season with salt and pepper to taste. Chill until ready to serve.

Serves 8.

Hoppin' John Salad

This is a salad version of the black-eyed pea and rice dish I grew to love when I dined at Alfalfa during my college days in Lexington. Alfalfa is no longer in business, but its legacy lives on with this dish. It travels well, so it makes a great work lunch or potluck dish for a rice-friendly crowd. Of all the salads in this chapter, this one is the earthiest, but it's a frequently requested recipe. It pulls together dimensions of savory and light that might be missing from other salads, and it's a good choice for a cold plate addition. Serve it with crusty bread or whole-grain crackers and fruit.

SALAD

2 cups cooked brown basmati
   rice, cooled to room
   temperature
2 cans black-eyed peas, rinsed
   and drained
1 cup thinly sliced celery

1 cup chopped carrots
1 cup sliced green olives with
   jalapeno
1 large red or green bell
   pepper, seeded and diced
¼ cup chopped fresh parsley

¼ cup chopped fresh basil

1 shallot, minced

⅛–¼ teaspoon cayenne

DRESSING

¾ cup olive oil

¼ cup red wine vinegar

1 tablespoon lemon juice

1 teaspoon sea salt

Sea salt and freshly ground
black pepper to taste

Lemon wedges

Combine the salad ingredients in a large bowl and toss to thoroughly combine. To make the dressing, add olive oil, vinegar, lemon juice, and sea salt to a large measuring cup. Whisk to emulsify and pour over the salad. Taste for seasoning and add salt and pepper if needed. Serve with lemon wedges.

Serves 8–10.

Soups, Stews, and Chilis

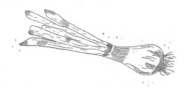

6

Soups, Stews, and Chilis

S oup takes center stage at my house. Even after a grueling day
at work, I can usually find the energy to chop some vegetables,
listen to Xavier Rudd or Caamp, and stir up a big pot of delicious herbs, spices, and vegetables that will rescue me from my
small-town vegan food desert for the next few days. Summertime
favorites are vegetable chowder and hearty vegetable soup to
take advantage of the abundance of fresh produce available. In
the cooler months, chilis and creamy potato or tomato soup are
included in the weekly rotation, with the occasional pasta with
bean soup thrown in to shake things up.

Just like salads, soups are malleable. They allow you to consider what ingredients you have on hand, who you're serving, and
your personal preference when it comes to a dominant flavor profile. They're also easy to tinker with and adjust on the fly should
some rowdy garlic or pepper try to steal the show. And they
are, of course, nutritional powerhouses. So stir quietly, breathe
deeply, and enjoy.

Vegetable Chowder

Be warned: you won't be able to eat just one bowl of this soup. The first time I had this chowder at my friend Julie's house, I was embarrassed by the amount I consumed. Fortunately for me, she was familiar with my appetite for vegetables, so she made a big pot. Soon after, I cooked this soup for my friend Gerry, who confessed to pulling off the road to eat the extra bowl I had sent home with her. She lived only twenty-five minutes away, and I remain perplexed about what kind of utensil she used to polish it off, thinking it best not to ask. This simple but delicious blend of vegetables highlights the best of summer corn. Better make a double batch.

½ stick vegan butter
2 cups chopped celery
1 onion, chopped
3 tablespoons chopped green
    pepper
1 14.5-ounce can stewed
    tomatoes, pureed
2 cups fresh corn
1 teaspoon sea salt
¼ teaspoon freshly ground
    black pepper

¼ teaspoon paprika
½ cup whole cashews
½ cup filtered water
1½ cups vegetable broth
½ cup shredded vegan
    cheddar
3 tablespoons unbleached all-
    purpose flour
½ cup chopped pimento

Melt the vegan butter in a large pot over medium heat. Add the celery, onion, and green pepper and sauté for 10 minutes, or until the onion is translucent. Stir in the pureed tomatoes, corn, salt, pepper, and paprika. Simmer for 30 minutes. Remove from the heat and set aside. In a high-speed blender, combine the cashews, filtered water, and vegetable broth. Blend at high speed for 1–2 minutes, or until smooth. Add the shredded cheddar and blend an additional 1 minute. Add the flour to the blender mixture and blend for 1–2 minutes, until smooth and creamy. Stir the cheese mixture into the soup, along with the pimento. Return to the heat and stir until the soup is heated through and thick. Serve immediately.

Serves 8.

Chili

This recipe has a long list of ingredients, but I promise that once you assemble them, it's a piece of cake. I love the flavor of fire-roasted tomatoes, and the carrots and corn perfectly balance the tomatoes' acidity to create a savory dish that's irresistible. It's delightful to catch the scent of this chili wafting from the window on a fall day. Top it with some vegan sour cream and scallions, or pair it with a green salad and cornbread for dinner. Use any leftovers for chili, cheese, and slaw dogs.

½ cup olive oil

1 large onion, chopped

4 stalks celery, chopped

2 tablespoons chopped garlic

½ teaspoon crushed red pepper flakes

2 teaspoons ground cumin

2 teaspoons dried oregano

3 tablespoons dark chili powder

2 28-ounce cans fire-roasted crushed tomatoes

2 15-ounce cans black beans, rinsed and drained

5 cups water

1 cup vegan India pale ale (IPA), or an additional 1 cup water

1 cup coarsely chopped carrots

1 cup fresh or frozen corn

3 bell peppers (1 red, 1 green, 1 yellow), diced

⅓ cup finely chopped fresh parsley

1 tablespoon sea salt

½ teaspoon freshly ground black pepper

1 cup cooked brown rice

1 12-ounce package browned vegan beef-style crumbles (optional)

Heat the oil in a large pot over medium heat. Add the onion, celery, and garlic and sauté for 5–7 minutes, or until the onions are translucent. Add the red pepper flakes, cumin, oregano, and chili powder and stir for 1–2 minutes, until fragrant. Stir in the fire-roasted tomatoes, black beans, water, and IPA and bring to a simmer. Add the carrots, corn, bell peppers, and parsley and simmer, stirring occasionally, for 1 hour over medium-low heat. Remove from the heat and stir in the salt, pepper, rice, and crumbles. Allow to sit for 10 minutes before serving.

Serves 10.

Bean Soup

Pintos are soft beans that easily release starch into the cooking liquid, ensuring a creamy, rich soup. This thick, savory base is what we Appalachians call bean soup or "soup beans." Served with cornbread, fried potatoes, and cooked greens or slaw, it's a staple in many households. We also like to load up a big bowl of bean soup topped with onions, kraut, or chowchow and crumble some bread right in the bowl. This is a good hearty meal when the budget is tight. For only a few dollars and a little tweaking of the recipe, you can eat with Appalachian gusto for days. Leftovers can be served over rice with peppers, onions, and tomatoes, used in tacos, or whipped into Spicy Bean Dip (see chapter 4).

16 ounces pinto beans, rinsed and soaked overnight in 1 tablespoon sea salt	8 cups water
	1 large potato, peeled and halved
2 tablespoons olive oil	1 teaspoon liquid smoke
1 large onion, chopped	Freshly ground black pepper to taste
2 teaspoons smoked sea salt	

Rinse and drain the beans and set aside. Add the olive oil to a large pot over medium-high heat. Add the onions and sauté for 10 minutes, or until translucent. Add the beans and salt and stir to coat. Add the water, potato, and liquid smoke. Bring to a boil, reduce heat, and simmer for 1½–2 hours, stirring frequently to prevent sticking. Remove from the heat and test the beans for tenderness. Place the cooked potato halves and 1 cup beans in a blender and puree until smooth. Stir the puree back into the soup and heat through. Adjust seasonings to taste.

Serves 8.

Creamy Potato Soup

Cream of potato soup was the first soup I ever attempted to make. I was only fourteen, and I remember being very pleased with the somewhat watery results. It probably wasn't very good, but it was a confidence builder. Many years down the road, and with much improvement in the recipe development department, potato soup remains one of my favorites, especially as a one-dish meal. It's extremely filling, and I incorporate colorful vegetables and parsley to enhance the flavor and texture. It also happens to be the favorite soup of a handsome guitar player I know. So making an extra batch can't hurt.

3–4 pounds potatoes, peeled and diced into small cubes

¼ cup extra virgin olive oil

4 stalks celery, chopped

1 large onion, chopped

1 tablespoon minced garlic

1 bay leaf

32 ounces no-chicken broth

3 cups water, divided

2 teaspoons smoked sea salt

2 large carrots, halved lengthways and sliced into half moons

½ cup raw whole cashews

4 ounces shredded vegan cheddar

1 tablespoon nutritional yeast

¼ cup vegan butter

2 tablespoons unbleached all-purpose flour

¼ cup chopped flat-leaf parsley, plus additional for garnish

½ teaspoon freshly ground black pepper

1 6-ounce package smoked tempeh, cooked and crumbled

2 scallions, chopped

Place the potatoes in sufficient cold water to cover them completely, and set aside. Add olive oil to a large pot over medium-low heat. Add the celery, onion, garlic, and bay leaf and reduce heat to low to prevent overbrowning the garlic. Simmer for 10 minutes, or until the onions are translucent. Stir the broth and 2 cups water into the pot, add the potatoes, and bring to a boil. Add the sea salt and reduce the heat to simmer. Cook, stirring occasionally, for 30 minutes. Add the carrots and simmer for 20 more minutes. While the soup simmers, place the cashews, 1 cup water, vegan cheddar, nutritional yeast, vegan butter, and flour in a high-speed blender. Blend until completely smooth. Add this mixture, along with the parsley and black pepper, to the soup and stir until heated through. Add half the smoked tempeh crumbles to the soup. Remove from the heat and allow to sit for 10 minutes. Discard the bay leaf. Serve topped with scallions, the remaining tempeh, and additional parsley.

Serves 8.

Creamy Tomato Soup

No child of my era grew up without consuming their fair share of Campbell's soup. So I needed a vegan replacement for my personal favorite—cream of tomato—and this is it. When you feel like putting on your PJs and fuzzy socks and curling up with a good book or binge-watching *Virgin River*, this is the soup for you. Pour it in a cup, top it with some garlicky croutons, and get yourself a blanket. I could just as easily call it cozy time in a bowl. For a substantial lunch, have it with an eggless tofu salad sandwich on whole-grain bread. Maybe this replacement will eliminate that annoying Campbell's jingle from my memory. If you don't know what that is, consider yourself lucky.

¼ cup olive oil	½ teaspoon dried savory
1 medium onion, chopped	½ teaspoon dried dill
1 large carrot, chopped	½ teaspoon dried thyme
2 stalks celery, chopped	1 28-ounce can fire-roasted
2 bay leaves	crushed tomatoes
1 tablespoon chopped garlic	4 cups no-chicken broth
¼ cup tomato paste	2 teaspoons sugar, divided

2 teaspoons salt
½ teaspoon freshly ground
   black pepper

½ cup vegan sour cream
Salt and black pepper to taste

Heat the olive oil in a large pot over medium heat. Add the onion, carrot, celery, and bay leaves and sauté for 10 minutes, until the vegetables are soft and the onion is translucent. Add the garlic, tomato paste, savory, dill, and thyme and cook, stirring frequently, for another 10 minutes. Add the tomatoes, broth, 1 teaspoon sugar, salt, and pepper. Bring the soup to a boil, reduce the heat, and simmer for 1 hour. Allow the soup to cool and remove the bay leaves. Working in small batches, puree the soup in a blender until smooth. Return the pureed soup to the large pot and stir in the vegan sour cream. Simmer the soup for 10 minutes, until the flavors meld, stirring frequently to prevent sticking. Season to taste with salt, pepper, and the remaining 1 teaspoon sugar if desired.

Serves 4.

Farmhouse Stew

This hearty mushroom-based stew is a favorite of my sons, so I have been making it for years with only minor changes to the original recipe. It pairs well with cornbread and a green salad. We sometimes just spoon the stew over the cornbread and top it with a dollop of vegan sour cream. It makes a nice one-plate presentation for an easy weeknight dinner. This recipe calls for seitan, but vegan beef tips also work nicely.

2 cups seitan chunks
2 tablespoons olive oil,
   divided
6 medium potatoes, peeled
   and cut into a large dice
4 large carrots, peeled and
   sliced into 1-inch chunks

2 bay leaves
2 cups vegetable broth
1½ cups water, divided
1 large onion, chopped
2 stalks celery, finely chopped
2 teaspoons minced garlic
½ teaspoon dried thyme

½ teaspoon dried marjoram
8 ounces white mushrooms, cleaned and very finely chopped
½ cup dry white wine

2 tablespoons unbleached all-purpose flour
2 tablespoons tahini
3 tablespoons tamari
Sea salt and freshly ground black pepper

Preheat oven to 400 degrees. Toss the seitan chunks with 1 tablespoon olive oil and spread on a nonstick baking sheet. Bake for 15 minutes until just starting to brown. Remove from the oven and set aside. Place the potatoes, carrots, and bay leaves in a large stockpot with the vegetable broth and 1 cup water. Bring to a boil, reduce heat to medium, cover, and simmer for 20 minutes, or until the vegetables are tender. Place the remaining 1 tablespoon oil in a large skillet over medium-high heat. Add the onion, celery, garlic, thyme, and marjoram and sauté for 8–10 minutes, until the vegetables are tender. Add the mushrooms and white wine and continue to cook, stirring frequently, for another 6–8 minutes. Remove the skillet from the heat, stir in the flour and tahini, and mix will. Add the remaining ½ cup water and tamari and stir until the mixture is smooth. Add the mushroom mixture to the hot cooked vegetables in the stockpot, stir in the seitan, and bring the stew to a boil. Stir continuously until the liquid thickens, about 5 minutes. Remove the bay leaves and season with salt and pepper. Serve hot.

Serves 8.

Hearty Vegetable Soup

This is the soup I turn to when it's been a long day and I need to unwind. Quietly chopping and stirring allows me to destress, and my mood is immediately lifted by the comforting aroma of garlic and herbs. This recipe lists the ingredients I usually include, but honestly, I typically just start with some olive oil, garlic, and onion and chop up whatever I have on hand. So don't let the lack of one or two vegetables discourage you from trying this soup.

It's an ultra-forgiving recipe and an opportunity to use whatever's fresh in your kitchen. Light some candles, queue up the Head and the Heart, and start chopping!

¼ cup extra virgin olive oil

1 large onion, chopped

1 tablespoon chopped garlic

2 stalks celery, finely chopped

1 bay leaf

1 28-ounce can fire-roasted chopped tomatoes

8 cups water

2 cups thinly sliced carrots

2 cups potatoes, peeled and diced

1 cup fresh or frozen corn

1 cup baby spinach, destemmed and cut into ribbons

1 can garbanzo beans, rinsed and drained

¼ cup chopped flat-leaf parsley

2 teaspoons sea salt

½ teaspoon freshly ground black pepper

½ teaspoon dried basil

½ teaspoon dried oregano

½ cup cooked brown rice

Sea salt and freshly ground black pepper to taste

Heat the olive oil in a large stockpot over medium heat. Add the onion, garlic, celery, and bay leaf. Sauté for 6–8 minutes, or until the onion is translucent. Add the rest of the ingredients, except for the rice. Bring the soup to a boil, reduce the heat, and simmer, stirring occasionally, for 1 hour. Stir in the rice and heat through. Remove the bay leaf and adjust the seasonings, if needed. Serve immediately. Leftovers will keep for several days covered and refrigerated.

Serves 8.

Pasta with Bean Soup

The night after I first made this soup, everyone returned home from work with the same idea: leftovers! Unfortunately, the first person who got home stole the prize, and he had quite a hearty appetite. There wasn't a drop left for the rest of us. My son's fiancée was the most disappointed to see Cody's empty bowl and Cheshire Cat smile. I made another pot the next week just to keep the peace.

1½ cups navy beans, soaked overnight

10 cups water

4 tablespoons extra virgin olive oil, divided

¼ cup nutritional yeast

5 teaspoons chopped garlic, divided

2 medium carrots, halved crosswise

2 stalks celery, halved crosswise

½ teaspoon crushed red pepper flakes

6 sprigs fresh parsley

2 bay leaves

1 sprig fresh rosemary

1 large onion, chopped

1 28-ounce can fire-roasted crushed tomatoes

¾ cup dry white wine

1 cup lasagna broken into 1½-inch pieces

¼ cup chopped flat-leaf parsley

1 cup chopped baby kale

Salt and pepper to taste

Bring the beans, water, 1 tablespoon olive oil, nutritional yeast, 3 teaspoons garlic, carrots, celery, red pepper flakes, parsley, bay leaves, and rosemary to a boil in a large pot. Reduce heat to medium, cover, and simmer, stirring occasionally, for 1½ hours, or until the beans are tender. Remove from the heat, season with salt and pepper, and let sit for 30 minutes. Remove the vegetables, herbs, and bay leaves and discard them.

Meanwhile, in a medium pot, heat the remaining 3 table-spoons olive oil. Add the onion and cook for 8–10 minutes, or until soft and translucent. Add the tomatoes and cook, stirring often, for 15 minutes to reduce the liquid. Add the wine, bring to a boil, and continue to cook for an additional 5 minutes, until the liquid is almost evaporated. Stir the tomato mixture into the beans and broth and simmer 15 minutes. Add the lasagna and cook, stirring frequently, until the pasta is al dente, about 15 minutes. Add the parsley and kale and cook 1 minute longer.

Remove from the heat, season with salt and pepper, and allow to sit covered for 15 minutes. Serve topped with a drizzle of olive oil and red pepper flakes.

Serves 6.

White Chick'n Chili

I thought this dish was exotic the first time I had it. Everyone's family had chili, but this creamy white version was a new experience for me. My ambivalence was easily overcome by its cheesy goodness and spicy green specks of flavor. Soon, this recipe and other versions of it took the whole town by storm. It seemed that everyone and their sister had a pot of white chili on the stove. I even remember making it in home economics class. The trendy avocado topping is a new addition to prove that I can roll with the times.

1 12-ounce package vegan chick'n tenders

¼ cup plus 1 tablespoon olive oil, divided

1 large onion, chopped

2 stalks celery, chopped

4 teaspoons chopped garlic

1 teaspoon dried oregano

¼ teaspoon crushed red pepper flakes

1 cup dry white wine

5 cups no-chicken broth, divided

2 cups water

1 cup potatoes, peeled and diced

1 cup fresh or frozen corn

1 can great northern beans, rinsed and drained

1 4-ounce can chopped green chilis

1 teaspoon cumin

½ teaspoon garlic powder

½ teaspoon onion powder

1 tablespoon tamari

½ cup whole raw cashews, soaked overnight

Filtered water

1 block jack-style vegan cheese, cut into small cubes

2 tablespoons chopped flat-leaf parsley

2 tablespoons chopped
   cilantro, plus additional for
   garnish
Sea salt and freshly ground
   black pepper to taste

2 limes
4 scallions, chopped
1 avocado, diced

Preheat oven to 350 degrees. Toss the vegan chick'n pieces with
1 tablespoon olive oil and place on a nonstick baking sheet. Bake
for 15–20 minutes, until they start to brown, and allow to cool
before dicing into small pieces. Heat ¼ cup olive oil in a large
stockpot over medium heat. Add the onion and celery and sauté
for 8 minutes, or until the onion is translucent. Add the garlic,
oregano, and red pepper flakes and cook for another 4 minutes.
Add the wine and simmer for 10 minutes, stirring occasionally.
Add 4 cups broth, water, potatoes, corn, northern beans, green
chilis, cumin, garlic powder, onion powder, and tamari and bring
to a boil. Reduce heat and simmer for 1 hour. Meanwhile, rinse
and drain the soaked cashews and place them in a high-speed
blender with enough filtered water to cover. Add the remaining
1 cup broth and vegan cheese and blend at high speed until completely smooth. Stir the cashew mixture into the soup, along with
the parsley and cilantro, and heat through. Season with sea salt
and freshly ground black pepper. Squeeze the juice of 1 lime into
the soup and stir to combine. Slice the second lime into wedges.
Serve the chili topped with scallions, avocado, and additional
cilantro, with lime wedges on the side.

Serves 8.

Navy Bean Soup

My elementary school cafeteria used to serve a bland version of
this soup made with, I'm guessing, beans, salt, and water. Naturally, we did what any resourceful second graders would do to spice it
up: we added lots of ketchup. There is nothing visually appealing
about a lunch table full of kids eating ketchup soup. However, I
give us points for early palate development. This adaptation is

fresh and flavorful, and the diced tomatoes will satisfy anyone's latent ketchup urges.

1 pound navy beans, rinsed and soaked overnight

¼ cup olive oil

1 large onion, chopped

3 stalks celery, chopped

1 tablespoon chopped garlic

½ teaspoon dried savory

½ teaspoon dried basil

8 cups water

1 cup finely chopped carrots

1 cup baby kale, destemmed and coarsely chopped

1 14.5-ounce can fire-roasted diced tomatoes with juice

¼ cup fresh parsley

1 teaspoon liquid smoke

Sea salt and freshly ground black pepper to taste

Add the olive oil to a large stockpot over medium heat. Add the onion and celery and sauté for 8 minutes. Add the garlic, savory, and basil and cook for another 5 minutes. Add the drained and rinsed beans to the vegetables and stir to coat. Add the water, carrots, kale, tomatoes, parsley, and liquid smoke and bring to a boil. Reduce heat and simmer for 1½–2 hours, until the beans are tender. Puree 1 cup of soup in a blender and then stir it back into the pot. Season to taste with salt and pepper.

Serves 8.

Main Courses

7

Main Courses

My grandmother Elva, like many Appalachian mamas, was no dilettante when it came to cautionary tales. Ready to grab a gunny sack and join the fun at the town's new amusement park slide? Beware of razor blades on the descent! Going out to saddle up your new pony? Did you hear about the little girl down the road whose face was bitten "clean off" by her tiny flesh-eating steed? But Elva's kitchen—perhaps because it was her comfort zone—was a warning-free, no-holds-barred exploratorium. If I wanted to use the electric mixer at high speed or bake at 450 degrees—no problem. My grandmother's method of dealing with annoying questions was her own cleverly designed precursor to the white-noise machine. She might sit herself down at the sewing machine and treadle away or sit down at the piano and play really loudly. Her choice of activity was dictated by the decibel level she required, which in turn was dependent on the number of grandchildren who happened to be visiting. Any and all questions were acknowledged by a head nod, a smile, and an increase in volume. I interpreted this noncommittal response as a directive to figure it out for myself. This experience proved especially useful when it came to creating the dishes in this chapter.

Our hearts and minds retain an indelible impression of the regional foods we grew up with. My lifestyle choice meant using my vegan tool kit to revamp those culinary mainstays, and I wanted to get it right. Cashew crème, olive oil, mushrooms, tamari, nutritional yeast, cooking wines, and vinegars all add depth of flavor and contribute to the right balance of salt, fat, and acid. If you're looking for a savory pot pie, a flavorful one-dish pasta meal, or something meaty and substantial to pair with your favorite vegetables, you've come to the right chapter.

Swiss Seitan

For most of us, there's one special food that conjures up warm childhood memories. Maybe something noteworthy happened that forever locks that meal into a positive sensory space, or maybe it was your family's go-to meal for special occasions. I like to re-create these special meals à la vegan for my friends. Unluckily for me, one friend's comfort meal happened to be Swiss steak. Why not a nice scalloped potato and onion dish or a creamy pasta? Nonetheless, challenge accepted! With just a little research, this recipe came together easily. After consuming the requested meal of Swiss seitan, mashed potatoes, skillet corn, slaw, green beans, and dinner rolls, my recipe tester decided there was no need for dessert after all and promptly fell asleep. Success! Vegan beef tips can stand in for the seitan. This recipe is also delicious served over rice with a side salad.

16 ounces traditionally prepared seitan

¼ cup unbleached all-purpose flour

¾ teaspoon sea salt

½ teaspoon freshly ground black pepper

4 tablespoons olive oil, divided

1 onion, chopped

1 tablespoon chopped garlic

½ cup chopped green bell pepper

1 14.5-ounce can diced tomatoes

2 tablespoons tomato paste

½ cup vegetable broth

1 tablespoon cooking sherry

1 teaspoon vegan Worcestershire sauce

½ cup finely chopped fresh parsley, plus additional for garnish

½ teaspoon paprika

In a large bowl, whisk together the flour, salt, and pepper. Toss the seitan in the flour mixture until evenly coated. In a medium skillet, heat 2 tablespoons olive oil over medium-high heat. Add the seitan to the hot skillet and cook until evenly browned on all sides. Remove the seitan from the skillet and set aside. Reduce the heat to medium-low and add the remaining 2 tablespoons olive oil to the skillet. Stir in the onion, garlic, and bell pepper and sauté for 5–7 minutes. Add the remaining ingredients and simmer for 30 minutes. Stir in the seitan and taste for seasoning. Garnish with additional parsley.

Serves 6.

Spaghetti with Marinara

I know what you're thinking. In a *Family Feud* survey of Appalachian foods, spaghetti wouldn't be one of the top five answers on the board. Steve Harvey would be much more likely to shout out, "Survey says—cornbread!" or "fried chicken!" But every family I knew as a child served some version of spaghetti. I was a loosely supervised neighborhood wanderer, so although my survey was not official, it was extensive.

Naturally, I was curious about this apparent menu anomaly, and it didn't take much research to discover that many Italians from the poorer region of southern Italy migrated to mountain states like Kentucky between 1800 and 1920 to take jobs in the railroad and coal mining industries. Canned tomatoes were readily available, and spaghetti (never a truly authentic Sicilian main course) took on an American life of its own. We've been churning it out and calling it Italian ever since.

This recipe leaves no one behind. On a recent trip to Florida with some of my favorite people, I wanted to make a celebratory dinner, and my friend's sister was adamant that she didn't want "health food." Although the sauce boasts a total of seven fresh herbs and vegetables, the presentation is familiar, and it's a far cry from trotting out a lentil loaf. To mask the vegetables and protect the sensibilities of those who might object to the sight of an intact mushroom, let the sauce cool, puree it in a blender, stir in the vegan crumbles, and reheat. For our celebratory dinner in Florida, I added a loaf of garlic bread and a salad and whipped out the Ben and Jerry's vegan ice cream topped with Oreos and chocolate sauce for dessert. All comfort zones remained fully intact.

½ cup plus 2 tablespoons
   extra virgin olive oil,
   divided
1 onion, chopped
½ teaspoon crushed red
   pepper flakes
1 green bell pepper, diced
8 ounces white mushrooms,
   thinly sliced
2 tablespoons minced garlic
2 28-ounce cans fire-roasted
   crushed tomatoes

1 cup water
¼ cup chopped fresh parsley
¼ cup chopped fresh basil
1 teaspoon dried oregano
1 teaspoon sea salt
1 10-ounce package ground
   vegan crumbles (optional)
Freshly ground black pepper
   to taste
1 pound spaghetti

Heat ½ cup olive oil over medium-high heat in a large skillet or saucepan. Add onion and cook for 10 minutes, or until the onion is translucent. Add red pepper flakes, bell pepper, mushrooms, and garlic and simmer for an additional 10 minutes. Add tomatoes, water, parsley, basil, oregano, and sea salt; lower the heat to medium-low; and cook for 45–60 minutes, stirring occasionally. While the sauce is simmering, brown the crumbles in 2 tablespoons olive oil. Cook the spaghetti in salted water according to package directions. Stir the browned crumbles into the sauce and cook for an additional 5 minutes. Pour the cooked pasta into a serving dish and spoon the sauce over the top. Serve with crusty bread and a green salad.

Serves 8.

Mama Mac

During my earliest years, I spent a lot of time with my aunt Mary Lou. She was an elementary school teacher and had a special gift for storytelling. I loved to listen to her describe her life growing up. One time, she told me a story about my uncle Ted's grandparents: They set out in their VW Beetle and headed to nearby Richmond, Kentucky, the closest shopping destination. If you have ever traveled Highway 52, you know that much of it is sliced right out of the mountain, and rock slides are not uncommon. Midway through the trip, a loose boulder bounced down the mountainside and landed on the hood of the Beetle. Aunt Mary Lou could have stopped the story right there, and I would have been happy with the singular image of Mama and Daddy Mack sitting in their VW with a giant rock as a hood ornament. But there was shopping to do, so they simply turned around, cruised back to town with the rock still on the hood, parked the VW in the driveway, and took another car to Richmond. For me, that story has always been the definition of perseverance. I named this dish after Mama Mack because it has her spice and staying power, and with its familiar flavors and textures, it's a rock-solid choice to please any dinner guest who might show up. It's best made and served the same day.

¾ cup nutritional yeast

⅓ cup pine nuts

2 teaspoons onion powder

1 teaspoon garlic powder

½ teaspoon salt

1 tablespoon dried parsley

1 teaspoon freshly ground
   black pepper

1 tablespoon tamari

1 cup no-chicken broth

4 ounces vegan cheddar,
   grated

3 tablespoons extra virgin
   olive oil

¼ cup all-purpose flour

12 ounces elbow macaroni

1 14-ounce can diced
   tomatoes

½ cup whole wheat
   breadcrumbs

Fresh parsley for garnish

Preheat oven to 350 degrees. Place the nutritional yeast, pine nuts, onion powder, garlic powder, salt, parsley, and black pepper in a high-speed blender and process until finely ground. Add the tamari, broth, and vegan cheddar and process until completely smooth. Add the olive oil and flour to the cheese mixture and process again (the blender's soup speed works well here). Cook the macaroni according to package directions and drain well. Combine the macaroni, tomatoes, and cheese mixture in a large casserole dish and top with the breadcrumbs. Bake 30–40 minutes, or until the breadcrumbs are browned and the mixture is bubbly. Top with fresh parsley and serve with a green salad and crusty bread.

Serves 8–10.

Fried Chick'n

Before going to pharmacy school, I attended Eastern Kentucky University for two years. There was no cooking allowed in the dorm (hide those hotplates!), so Ma Kelly's was our favorite destination when we felt homesick and needed some comfort food. Health inspections were significantly more relaxed in the 1970s, and Ma's was basically just a house. You grabbed a plate and waded right into the middle of the cooking action so Ma and her staff could serve you the delicious home-cooked entrée of the day accompanied by lots of mashed potatoes and veggies. Ma herself would later wander by your table, take a gander at your plate, and verbally tell you the price of your meal. This is my vegan version of her fried chicken. I still love it with mashed potatoes, green beans, and warm rolls on the side.

2 10-ounce packages frozen Gardien chick'n scallopini or any nonbreaded chicken substitute
2 tablespoons sea salt, divided
2 teaspoons plus 1 tablespoon freshly ground black pepper, divided
1½ teaspoons paprika
¾ teaspoon cayenne
½ teaspoon garlic powder
½ teaspoon onion powder
1 cup unsweetened soy milk
2 teaspoons apple cider vinegar
1 tablespoon vegan egg whisked in ½ cup very cold water
3 cups flour
1 tablespoon cornstarch
Peanut oil for frying

Remove the frozen chick'n patties from the package. Combine 1 tablespoon sea salt, 2 teaspoons black pepper, paprika, cayenne, garlic powder, and onion powder and rub both sides of the patties with the mixture. Place the patties back in freezer. Combine the soy milk and vinegar and set aside to thicken. Add the vegan egg mixture to the thickened milk, combine well, and place in a shallow bowl. Whisk together the flour, 1 tablespoon sea salt, 1 tablespoon black pepper, and cornstarch and place in a second shallow bowl. Remove the patties from the freezer, dip them in the milk mixture, and then roll them in the flour mixture, completely covering all sides. Pour ¾–1 inch peanut oil in a large skillet over medium-high heat. When the oil is hot, place the patties in the skillet 4 at a time, reduce heat to medium, and fry 4–6 minutes on each side, until crispy and golden brown. Serve hot.

Serves 8.

Meatloaf

Along with Swiss steak, meatloaf is one of my omnivorous friends' favorite meals. There are many varieties of vegan ground round available, but my first choice is the Impossible brand. In a pinch, you can thaw 4 vegan burgers and mix them together before adding the other ingredients and seasonings. I like to pair this main course with mashed potatoes and gravy along with something green, such as steamed broccoli or asparagus, and a salad component, such as a tangy slaw or brined cucumbers. Save some brined cucumbers to add to a cold meatloaf sandwich the next day. The glaze is optional, but it's a popular addition.

LOAF

- 1 pound vegan ground round
- 1 green bell pepper, finely diced
- 1 medium onion, finely chopped
- 1 tablespoon minced garlic
- 1 tablespoon extra virgin olive oil
- 6 ounces tomato paste
- 1 tablespoon vegan Worcestershire sauce
- ½ cup Just Egg or other liquid egg replacer

1½ cups whole-grain
    breadcrumbs
¾ teaspoon sea salt

½ teaspoon freshly ground
    black pepper

GLAZE

¾ cup ketchup
1 tablespoon white vinegar
3 tablespoons brown sugar
1 teaspoon garlic powder

½ teaspoon onion powder
¼ teaspoon black pepper
¼ teaspoon salt

Preheat oven to 350 degrees. Line a 9-inch loaf pan with nonstick foil and set aside. Add the bell pepper, onion, and garlic to the vegan ground round. In a small bowl, mix the olive oil, tomato paste, Worcestershire sauce, and liquid vegan egg and pour over the loaf mixture. Add the breadcrumbs, salt, and pepper and use your hands to incorporate the ingredients and form into a loaf. Place the loaf in the prepared pan, cover with foil, and bake for 30 minutes. Remove the foil and bake for an additional 10–15 minutes, until the top is nicely browned. Combine all the glaze ingredients and spread evenly over the loaf. Serve warm. Leftovers will keep for 3 days.

Serves 6.

Shepherd's Pie

During my first year of pharmacy school, I shared an apartment in Lexington with my longtime bestie ML. It was a busy and stressful year, with little time for cooking. But, armed with our pocket-size Betty Crocker cookbook and a hotline to ML's mother for cooking advice, we managed to prepare some delicious meals in our tiny kitchen. One of our favorites, maybe because it was so cheap, was a deep-dish hamburger pie. Our college legacy lives on in this spiced-up vegan version. If you prefer, a layer of cooked lentils can stand in for the seitan.

4 tablespoons olive oil, divided

2 8-ounce packages traditional seitan, finely chopped

1 onion, chopped

1 tablespoon chopped garlic

1 10-ounce package frozen kale

1 10-ounce package frozen corn

1 cup vegetable broth

¼ cup dry red wine or red cooking wine

1 teaspoon dried basil

1 teaspoon dried thyme

2 tablespoons tamari

3 tablespoons cornstarch

4½ teaspoons salt, divided

3 pounds Yukon Gold potatoes

½ cup unsweetened almond milk at room temperature

½ teaspoon freshly ground black pepper

¼ cup vegan butter at room temperature

¼ cup vegan sour cream

½ cup whole wheat breadcrumbs

2 teaspoons dried parsley

¼ cup vegan parmesan

Preheat oven to 350 degrees. Heat 2 tablespoons olive oil in a skillet over medium-high heat. Add the seitan and cook until lightly browned, about 7 minutes. Spread the seitan in the bottom of an oiled casserole dish. Add the remaining 2 tablespoons olive oil to the skillet, reduce heat to medium, and sauté the onion until translucent, about 5 minutes. Add the garlic, frozen kale, and frozen corn and simmer, stirring until the vegetables are just thawed. Layer the vegetables evenly over the seitan. Whisk together the broth, wine, tamari, basil, thyme, cornstarch, and 1 teaspoon salt. Pour the liquid mixture evenly over the casserole mixture. Peel the potatoes and cut them into quarters. Place the potatoes in a large pot, cover with water, and bring to a boil. Add 3 teaspoons salt to the boiling water and cook until the potatoes are tender when pierced with a fork, about 30 minutes. Drain the potatoes and steam them over the burner for a minute to remove the excess moisture; then use a potato masher or ricer to mash the hot potatoes. Stir in the almond milk, ½ teaspoon salt, and black pepper. Combine until smooth. Add the softened vegan butter and vegan sour cream and combine. Spread the potatoes evenly over the casserole mixture. Toss together the breadcrumbs, parsley, and vegan parmesan. Sprinkle the crumb mixture over the casserole and bake for 40 minutes, until the topping is lightly browned and the casserole is bubbly. Taste for seasoning. Serve hot.

Serves 8.

Country Fried Steak with Brown Gravy

This is a stick-to-the-ribs entrée, suitable for folks with hearty appetites or those who want to experience a vegan version of the traditional regional cuisine. There are numerous veggie burgers on the market, but for this dish, you want one that mimics the taste of beef (such as Boca or Beyond). I like to serve this dish with mashed potatoes, green beans, skillet corn, slaw, and cornbread. If it happens to be summertime, slice a couple of fresh tomatoes to serve on the side, topped with a little vinegar, salt, and pepper.

8 veggie burgers, thawed, shaped into 6 steaks, and sprinkled with salt and pepper

1½ cups unbleached all-purpose flour

1 teaspoon garlic powder

1 teaspoon onion powder

1 teaspoon dried thyme

1 teaspoon sea salt

1 teaspoon freshly ground black pepper

1 cup unsweetened soy milk

½ cup Just Egg liquid

½ teaspoon hot sauce

1 teaspoon vegan Worcestershire sauce

1 cup canola or grapeseed oil for frying

Brown Sauce/Gravy (see chapter 11)

Sift together the flour, garlic powder, onion powder, thyme, salt, and pepper and pour into a shallow bowl. In a separate bowl, whisk together the soy milk, Just Egg, hot sauce, and Worcestershire sauce. Dredge the burgers in the flour mixture, dip into the milk mixture, then dredge in the flour mixture again. Pat the steaks until completely coated with flour and set aside for 10–15 minutes. Heat the oil in a large skillet over medium-high heat. When the oil is hot, add the steaks 3 at a time. Fry 3–4 minutes on each side, until golden brown and crispy. Place on brown paper or paper towels to soak up the excess oil. Serve with brown gravy.

Serves 6.

Pot Roast Dinner

This is dinner made easy. Just throw everything in the pot, simmer, and enjoy the fragrance while you make a salad or sip a glass of wine. I can honestly say that my favorite part of this dish is the carrots. The red wine sauce gives them an incomparable flavor that can entice even hard-core carrot dissidents to get their beta-carotene. I like to serve this with a simple green salad and some crispy cornbread. However, if you want to gussy it up with some slaw, skillet corn, and mac and cheese, go right ahead.

2 tablespoons olive oil
1 pound traditional seitan or vegan beef tips
8 ounces white mushrooms, halved
2 bay leaves
1 teaspoon dried thyme
2 small sweet onions, cut into quarters
6 shallots, chopped
1 tablespoon minced garlic
1 pound baby carrots
1 pound small new potatoes, washed and scrubbed
½ cup vegetable broth
½ cup dry red wine
2 tablespoons tomato paste
2 tablespoons tamari
½ teaspoon black pepper
Sea salt to taste

Place the olive oil in a large stockpot over medium-high heat. Add the seitan or vegan beef tips and stir to coat with oil. Cook for 5 minutes, or until nicely browned. Remove from the pot and set aside. Add more olive oil if needed and return the stockpot to the heat. Stir in the mushrooms, bay leaves, thyme, onions, shallots, and garlic. Cook, stirring frequently, until the mushrooms begin to soften, about 5 minutes. Return the seitan to the pot, add the carrots and potatoes, and stir to combine. Whisk together the broth, wine, tomato paste, tamari, and black pepper. Pour the broth mixture into the pot and adjust the heat to medium-high. Bring the broth to a boil; then reduce to a simmer. Cover the pot and simmer for 1 hour, adding liquid if needed. Remove the bay leaves. Season with salt to taste. Arrange the roast and vegetables on a large platter and serve hot.

Serves 4–6.

Chick'n Pot Pie

I love a good pot pie that's warm and savory with lots of veggies and a crispy crust. The shallots and white wine take this dish a step beyond the ordinary, and the aroma as it bakes takes me to a happy place. I have included the ingredients for a crust, but this dish is also delicious topped with biscuits or a store-bought vegan puff pastry if you're short on time. Simply increase the baking temperature to 425 degrees if you choose one of these options.

CHICK'N

10 ounces nonbreaded chick'n

1 tablespoon olive oil

CRUST

2½ cups unbleached all-purpose flour

1 teaspoon sugar

1 teaspoon salt

2 sticks (1 cup) vegan butter

¼–½ cup ice water

FILLING

3 tablespoons olive oil

2 small shallots, finely chopped

3 carrots, thinly sliced on the bias

2 large potatoes, cubed

½ cup fresh or frozen peas

½ cup dry white wine or white
cooking wine

2 cups no-chicken broth

1 teaspoon dried thyme

5 teaspoons cornstarch
whisked with 2 tablespoons
cold water

¾ cup vegan half-and-half

½ teaspoon salt

½ teaspoon freshly ground
black pepper

2 tablespoons finely chopped
fresh parsley

Preheat oven to 400 degrees. Toss the chick'n with 1 tablespoon olive oil and bake on nonstick aluminum foil for 20 minutes. Set aside to cool; then chop into cubes. To make the crust, place the flour, sugar, and salt in the bowl of a food processor and pulse to combine. Cut the vegan butter into small pieces and add to the bowl. Pulse about 10 times, or until the mixture looks like coarse meal. Slowly drizzle the water into the mixture while pulsing until the dough holds together when pressed between two fingers. Shape into a large disc, wrap in wax paper, and refrigerate for at least 1 hour. While the dough is chilling, make the filling by heating 3 tablespoons olive oil in a large saucepan over medium heat. Add the shallots and cook for 4–5 minutes. Add the carrots, potatoes, and peas and stir to combine. Continue to cook for another 10 minutes, until the vegetables begin to soften. Stir in the wine and simmer until the liquid is reduced by half. Add the broth, thyme, and browned chick'n and cook for another 4 minutes. Add the cornstarch mixture and vegan half-and-half. Cook for an additional 5 minutes, stirring occasionally, until the mixture is thick and bubbly. Stir in the salt, pepper, and fresh parsley and pour into a casserole dish. Place the chilled dough on floured wax paper and roll into a rectangle. Place the dough on top of the casserole to cover completely, and use a sharp knife to trim the edges. Pierce the crust with a fork 10–15 times. Bake on the middle rack of the oven for 40 minutes, or until the crust is golden brown and the mixture is bubbly. Serve hot.

Serves 6.

Not Tuna Casserole

The 1970s was the decade of the casserole. Cookbooks and magazines touted these dishes as time savers for busy working parents, and they often sported bizarre toppings such as potato chips, breakfast cereals, and lots of Velveeta (a weekly purchase in our household). Having consumed so many of them, I find that a little piece of my culinary heart is still devoted to these one-dish meals. Naturally, when companies like Sophie's began producing a mock tuna, I felt compelled to trot out the old family recipe for tuna casserole. There's no tuna, no chips, and no Velveeta, but it's a keeper nonetheless.

2 6-ounce cans Sophie's vegan tuna, drained

8 ounces wide noodles or other vegan pasta, cooked according to package directions

2 tablespoons vegan butter

2 tablespoons chopped onion

1 green bell pepper, diced

1 8-ounce can sliced button mushrooms, drained and rinsed

½ recipe Basic Vegan Cheese Sauce (see chapter 11)

½ teaspoon onion powder

½ teaspoon garlic powder

½ cup whole wheat breadcrumbs

Preheat oven to 350 degrees. Stir the vegan tuna into the cooked pasta. In a small saucepan, melt the vegan butter over medium heat and add the onion, green pepper, and mushrooms. Cook, stirring frequently, for 5–7 minutes. Stir the cooked vegetables into the pasta. To the vegan cheese sauce, add the onion powder and garlic powder and whir in the blender until combined. Stir the cheese sauce into the pasta and pour into an oiled casserole dish. Top with the breadcrumbs and bake uncovered for 30 minutes, or until heated through. Serve hot.

Serves 6.

Beyond Belief Steak

In my years as a Saturday waitress at the stockyards, I had many memorable encounters with customers. One of the regulars, an especially sour fellow, comes to mind whenever I make this dish. Since we were open only one day a week for the Saturday sales, we didn't have an extensive menu. In fact, there was no actual menu, no notepad to take orders, and no cash register. We simply yelled the orders back to the cook and added up the total and tax in our heads. My dad, a math teacher turned principal, thought this unorthodox practice made perfect sense. Based on his unassailable logic, it spared him the cost of a cash register while honing his children's math skills. We had the standard fare of burgers, hot dogs, and grilled cheese, and my uncle arrived at 6:00 a.m. to prepare the plate-lunch special—a rotating choice of meats and two vegetable sides, along with salad or slaw and cornbread. Customers who didn't want the meat special could substitute a hamburger steak. Every week for at least two years, one farmer unfailingly asked what we had on special. I obediently listed the options, to which he always replied, "Give me the hamburger steak." One Saturday, fully embracing my cranky teenage disposition, I questioned the need to tell him the available options and even went so far as to suggest that perhaps he was waiting for hamburger steak to be the special so he could simply reply, "Give me the special." I reasoned that avoiding this weekly banter would be a practical time saver, but he did not appreciate my observation. However, going forward, he did cut to the chase, so mission accomplished. This easy recipe will please omnivores and herbivores alike. I serve it topped with a combination of grilled mushrooms, onions, and peppers or a creamy mushroom gravy. It pairs well with twice-baked potatoes, salad, and rolls or rosemary bread.

1 pound Beyond Meat or
   other ground round
   substitute

1 tablespoon olive oil, plus
   additional for frying
1 tablespoon A1 Sauce

1 tablespoon minced garlic

1 tablespoon tamari

1 teaspoon vegan
   Worcestershire sauce

1 teaspoon freshly ground
   black pepper

Mix 1 tablespoon olive oil, A1 Sauce, garlic, tamari, Worcester-shire sauce, and black pepper. Using your hands, thoroughly incorporate this mixture into the ground round and then shape the ground round into 4 ovals. Cover the bottom of a large non-stick skillet with olive oil and heat over medium heat. Cook the ovals 5–7 minutes on each side, until brown and slightly crisp on the outside. Serve with additional vegan steak sauce or topped with grilled veggies or mushroom sauce.

Serves 4.

Beans and Greens

Appalachians love beans, which are both good and good for you. Whether you slow-cook or pressure-cook the beans, a nicely textured bean dish makes a mighty fine meal. Thanks to my farm share I get lots of kale, so that is my green of choice, but others, including collards and Swiss chard, work just as well. Toss togeth-er a colorful blend of chopped peppers, scallions, cilantro, and tomatoes, top with vegan sour cream, break out the cornbread, and pat yourself on the back for creating such a beautiful and healthy meal.

2 cups uncooked brown
   basmati rice

3½ cups no-chicken broth,
   divided

2 cups cranberry beans

3 tablespoons olive oil,
   divided

1 bunch kale, washed and
   sliced into thin ribbons

2 teaspoons chopped garlic

¼ teaspoon red pepper flakes

1½ tablespoons red wine
   vinegar, plus additional for
   serving

½ cup diced green pepper

½ cup diced red pepper

½ cup yellow cherry or grape
   tomatoes, halved

½ cup thinly sliced scallions

2 tablespoons chopped fresh
  cilantro

Sea salt and freshly ground
  black pepper to taste

Vegan sour cream

Prepare the rice according to package directions using 3 cups broth instead of water. (If you're using a rice steamer, you may be able to reduce the broth to less than 3 cups.) Cook the beans according to package directions and set aside. Heat 2 tablespoons olive oil in a large skillet over medium heat. Add the kale, garlic, and red pepper flakes and stir until the kale begins to wilt. Add ½ cup broth and continue cooking for 5 minutes, until the kale is bright green and reduced. Turn the heat to low and stir in the cooked rice and red wine vinegar. Toss together the green and red peppers, tomatoes, scallions, cilantro, and the remaining 1 tablespoon olive oil. Sprinkle this vegetable mixture with a little red wine vinegar. Adjust the salt and pepper in the rice mixture. Place a layer of rice on each plate, top with a layer of beans, and garnish generously with the vegetable mixture. Top with vegan sour cream and serve with additional red wine vinegar.

Serves 6.

Breads

Breads

I hail from a long line of cornbread and biscuit makers. My grandmothers might have made the occasional batch of rolls or angel biscuits, but they generally left the yeast breads to the Rainbow Bread Company, so I have consumed my fair share of the brown-and-serve variety. My love of bread making may be a manifestation of the pharmacist in me. I'm fascinated by the alchemy of yeast, sugar, water, and flour transforming into something warm and irresistible. Since that first year I decided to bake multiple herbed loaves to fill my Christmas gift baskets, I have been hooked. Ironically, my grandmothers seemed baffled by baskets filled with homemade breads, cookies, jellies, and cheeses. It was thoughtful, they said, but I shouldn't worry because they truly had enough food at home. Note to self: there's a big perceptional generation gap when it comes to the giving of food baskets.

This chapter includes everything from biscuits and quick breads to fluffy yeast rolls. Pumpkin bread is one of my favorite things to bake, eat, and gift to others. The aroma of fresh rosemary bread is unequaled, and it's a great accompaniment to a savory pasta sauce. Don't be intimidated by the recipes that include yeast. It's far more forgiving than you think. Just make sure the yeast is fresh, and you will almost certainly be pleased with the results. Alchemy awaits you!

Fresh Strawberry Bread

I make this bread whenever fresh strawberries are in season. I eat a slice (or two) and promptly deliver the rest to my neighbors or my work crew to keep myself from going back for more. It's like receiving a warm strawberry hug when you remove this bread from the oven. The lemon zest keeps it from being overly sweet. If, by chance, you have a slice left the next day, it's equally good toasted and served with a little vegan butter.

½ cup unsweetened applesauce

½ cup canola oil

½ cup vegan sour cream

1 teaspoon pure vanilla extract

1 tablespoon egg replacer powder

1 cup unbleached all-purpose flour

½ cup whole wheat pastry flour

1 teaspoon cinnamon

½ teaspoon baking soda

½ teaspoon sea salt

1 tablespoon lemon zest

1½ cups sliced fresh strawberries

½ cup chopped pecans

1 tablespoon demerara sugar

Preheat oven to 350 degrees. Oil and flour a 9- by 5-inch loaf pan. Mix the applesauce, canola oil, vegan sour cream, vanilla, and egg replacer powder with an electric mixer at medium speed for 1–2 minutes, or until well blended. In a large bowl, whisk together both flours, cinnamon, baking soda, salt, and lemon zest. Pour the liquid mixture over the flour and stir until just combined. Stir in the strawberries and pecans and pour into the prepared pan. Smooth the surface of the mixture and sprinkle with the demerara sugar. Bake for 1 hour, or until a toothpick inserted in the center comes out clean. Cool on a wire rack for 15 minutes. Loosen the edges with a knife before removing from the pan. Serve warm or at room temperature.

Serves 8.

Jalapeno Corn Sticks

Sometimes I like to shake things up in the cornbread department, and I'm very fond of those cast-iron pans with individual servings shaped like tiny ears of corn. If you have some leftover jalapeno or corn from another dish, give this recipe a try. If you like, a banana pepper can take the place of the jalapeno. I enjoy these corn sticks with any type of barbecue or a bowl of pintos and fried potatoes. If you don't have a cast-iron skillet, you can pan fry them in a little olive oil and top with salsa and sour cream for an appetizer.

1 tablespoon vegan shortening
1 cup unsweetened soy milk
1 teaspoon apple cider vinegar
¾ cup self-rising cornmeal
¼ teaspoon sea salt
½ teaspoon Creole seasoning

½ cup fresh corn
1 small jalapeno, finely
  chopped
Dash liquid smoke
¼ cup shredded vegan
  cheddar

Preheat oven to 450 degrees. Use the vegan shortening to thoroughly grease the pan, making sure all the dimply areas of each corn stick are coated. Place the pan in the oven to preheat. Mix the vinegar in the soy milk and set aside to thicken. In a medium bowl, whisk together the cornmeal, salt, and Creole seasoning. Stir the thickened soy milk into the cornmeal until combined. Add the corn, jalapeno, liquid smoke, and shredded vegan cheddar and mix well. Carefully remove the heated pan from the oven and use an ice cream scoop to fill each stick with the batter. Bake for 20–25 minutes, or until golden brown. Remove from the oven and gently run a knife around each stick to ensure easy removal. Serve immediately.

Serves 4.

Cornbread Focaccia

Sometimes you just feel like having cornbread, even when the rest of the meal might not be cornbread-appropriate. So I came up with this version of cornbread dressed in its Sunday best. It's lovely to behold, and it satisfies your cornbread craving even when you aren't preparing traditional Appalachian fare. It's great as an appetizer drizzled with a little olive oil and served with a cocktail or a glass of wine, but the garnish and spices also make it a nice addition to a piccata or pasta dish. You can slice the leftovers into croutons and refrigerate for 1–2 days. Toss the croutons into a cast-iron skillet and bake at 400 degrees for 15 minutes. Use to garnish salad or soup.

2 tablespoons vegan shortening

1½ cups unsweetened soy milk

1 tablespoon apple cider vinegar

¼ cup whole wheat flour

1¼ cups plus 1 tablespoon self-rising cornmeal, divided

1 package rapid-rise yeast

½ teaspoon sea salt

1 teaspoon Italian seasoning

1 cup vegan parmesan, divided

10 grape tomatoes, halved

10 kalamata olives, halved

¼ cup thinly sliced red onion

1 tablespoon chopped fresh rosemary

Preheat oven to 425 degrees. Place the vegan shortening in a 10-inch cast-iron skillet and heat on low to melt the shortening. Add the vinegar to the soy milk and allow to thicken. Add the flour, 1¼ cups cornmeal, yeast, sea salt, Italian seasoning, and ½ cup vegan parmesan to the thickened soy milk mixture and stir until all the ingredients are incorporated. Add the remaining 1 tablespoon cornmeal to the skillet and increase the heat to medium-high. Stir continuously with a fork until the cornmeal is browned. Swirl the skillet to ensure that all sides are coated with cornmeal before pouring the batter into the skillet. Top with tomatoes, olives, onions, and rosemary. Bake in the oven for 30 minutes. Turn the oven on broil and broil until the top is browned. Cool for 5 minutes before slicing and serving.

Serves 6.

Zucchini Bread

There's an old vegan expression: when your farm share gives you too much zucchini (and it will), make zucchini bread. This was never one of my favorite breads or muffins until I came across a recipe that added wheat germ. I've enhanced it with cinnamon and pecans to hit all the right flavor notes. Vegetables in my bread? Yes, please.

3 cups unbleached all-purpose flour
1¼ cups toasted wheat germ
3 teaspoons baking powder
1 teaspoon sea salt
2 teaspoons cinnamon
1 cup chopped pecans
½ cup unsweetened applesauce

1 tablespoon vegan egg powder dissolved in ¾ cup very cold water
1¾ cups sugar
1 tablespoon pure vanilla extract
⅔ cup canola oil
3 cups grated zucchini

Preheat oven to 350 degrees. Grease and flour two 9- by 5-inch loaf pans and set aside. In a large bowl, whisk together the flour, wheat germ, baking powder, sea salt, cinnamon, and pecans until fully combined. With an electric mixer, mix the applesauce and vegan egg at medium speed until light and fluffy. Add the sugar and beat for an additional 2 minutes. Add the vanilla and canola oil and continue beating until the mixture is smooth. Add the flour mixture 1 cup at a time, beating well after each addition. Stir in the zucchini and divide the mixture evenly between the 2 loaf pans. Bake for 1 hour, or until the top is golden brown and a toothpick inserted in the center comes out clean.

Makes 2 loaves.

Refrigerator Potato Rolls for a Crowd

This is an easy, no-knead, foolproof dinner roll. I make these for large gatherings when I need to prep as much as possible ahead of time. They can be mixed the day before and shaped and baked when you're ready to serve. After their breakup, my nephew's former girlfriend turned up at Thanksgiving dinner, and when someone asked if they were back together, she replied, "Nope, I just came for the rolls." Obviously, they had remained friendly. Still, it's powerful testimony to the appeal of homemade bread.

2 medium-sized russet or
    golden potatoes, peeled
⅔ cup sugar
⅔ cup vegan shortening
2½ teaspoons salt
2 tablespoons vegan egg
    powder mixed in ¾ cup
    very cold water

4½ teaspoons active dry yeast
1⅓ cups warm water, divided
6 cups unbleached all-
    purpose flour
1 tablespoon vegan butter,
    melted

Cook the potatoes in boiling water for 10 minutes, or until fork tender. Drain, place the potatoes back in the pan, and hold it over the warm burner for a moment to release the moisture. Press the drained potatoes through a ricer or mash with a potato masher until smooth. Set 1 cup potatoes aside to cool. In a large bowl, cream the sugar and shortening. Add the cooled potatoes, salt, and vegan egg mixture and mix at medium speed until light and fluffy. In a separate bowl, dissolve the yeast in ⅔ cup warm water. Add a pinch of sugar to proof, and allow to sit for 2–3 minutes, until slightly bubbly. Add the yeast to the potato mixture and stir. Beat in 2 cups flour and the remaining water. Continue to add the flour 1 cup at a time until a soft dough forms. Shape the dough into a ball without kneading and place it in a bowl oiled with vegan butter. Turn the dough once to coat the top. Cover the dough tightly and refrigerate for up to 2 days.

When ready to serve, preheat the oven to 375 degrees and line three 9-inch cake pans with parchment paper. Punch the dough down and divide into 3 equal pieces. Roll each piece of dough into 15 balls (about the size of Ping-Pong balls) and arrange in the pans. Cover and let rise in a warm, draft-free place for 30–45 minutes, or until doubled in size. Brush with melted vegan butter and bake for 16–18 minutes, or until golden brown.

Serves 18–20.

Bread Machine Rosemary Bread

If I were to ask my sons which food best conjures the aroma of their childhood dinners, I think it would be this bread. It's a recipe I developed when I began growing a kitchen garden, and I have made countless loaves over the years. The scent of garlic and rosemary never disappoints. I mix the dough in a bread machine—a thing of beauty for busy working parents—but it's baked in the oven to obtain a perfect shape and a brown crust. I serve it with spaghetti or other pasta dishes, a salad main course, or simple meals that consist of an entrée and a green salad. I like to dip it in some fruity olive oil combined with balsamic vinegar. (Once when I drizzled the vinegar into the oil it miraculously rolled into a smiley face. Seriously, I have a photo.) Alternatively, you can't go wrong with some quality vegan butter if bread dipping isn't your style.

¾ cup unsweetened almond
  milk
1 tablespoon olive oil
2 cups unbleached all-
  purpose flour
1½ teaspoons yeast
½ teaspoon sea salt

2 teaspoons sugar
1 teaspoon crushed dried
  rosemary (or 1 tablespoon
  freshly chopped rosemary)
1 teaspoon Italian seasoning
2 teaspoons minced garlic

Combine all the ingredients in the pan of the bread machine in the order listed. Turn the machine on the rise setting to allow the dough to mix, knead, and rise. Most bread machines take about 1½ hours to complete the cycle. Preheat oven to 400 degrees. Shape the dough into a smooth round about 2 inches thick. Place the dough on a baking sheet lined with parchment paper or coated with cooking spray. If desired, brush the top of the dough with additional olive oil and fresh or dried rosemary. Bake for 15–20 minutes, or until golden brown.

Serves 4.

Skillet Cornbread

Cornbread is the quintessential Appalachian staple. We love it hot from a cast-iron skillet alongside some pinto beans and chopped onions or with a big plate of half-runner green beans and new potatoes. Although my grandmother was a renowned baker, it was my grandfather who donned the apron to make a batch of cornbread for Sunday dinner. The cooks in my family used a local brand of self-rising cornmeal, and except for the omission of eggs, I have stayed true to that recipe. Good cornbread is a blend of art and science, and it's a matter of considerable pride to be known for your cornbread-making skills. Naturally, I think mine is the best.

1½ cups unsweetened soy milk
1 tablespoon apple cider vinegar
2 tablespoons vegan shortening

1½ cups plus 1 tablespoon self-rising yellow or white cornmeal
¼ teaspoon sea salt
½ teaspoon liquid smoke

Preheat oven to 450 degrees. Add the vinegar to the soy milk and set aside to thicken. Melt the vegan shortening in a 9-inch cast-iron skillet over medium heat. Swirl the shortening in the skillet to fully coat the sides. Whisk together 1½ cups cornmeal and salt and stir it into the thickened milk, along with the liquid smoke. Whisk just until smooth and all the cornmeal is incorporated.

Sprinkle the remaining 1 tablespoon cornmeal into the hot skillet and stir with a fork until nicely browned. This lends a nice crispness to the outside of the bread. Immediately pour the batter into the hot skillet. Bake in the oven for 20–25 minutes, or until the top is golden brown. Remove the skillet from the oven and run a slender spatula beneath the bread to loosen it before inverting and placing it back in the oven to bake for an additional 5 minutes. Serve hot with vegan butter.

Serves 4–6.

Biscuits

Warm, fluffy, and right from the oven, the biscuit has a special place in every Appalachian heart. Most of us remember the recipes used by our mothers or grandmothers. Whether their biscuits were rolled out or the regional cathead drop variety, somewhere in our heritage there is almost certainly a memorable biscuit maker. Until my older son expressed an interest in learning how to make scratch biscuits, I never realized how strong the urge is to overhandle the dough. His first batch turned out perfect, but let's just say there were lots of words of caution between the mixing of the dough and the biscuits emerging from the oven. Remember, the dough doesn't have to be smooth and perfect. The biscuits will be lovelier and fluffier for your self-restraint.

2 teaspoons baking powder
1 teaspoon sea salt
2 cups unbleached all-
    purpose flour, plus more to
    flour the kneading surface

½ cup chilled vegan butter,
    plus 1 tablespoon melted
½ cup vegan sour cream
½ cup vegan half-and-half

Preheat oven to 425 degrees. Whisk together the baking powder, sea salt, and 2 cups flour. Cut the chilled ½ cup vegan butter into 1-tablespoon slices and add to the flour. Using a pastry cutter or your fingers, work the vegan butter into the dough until it resembles coarse meal. With a fork, mix in the vegan sour cream and vegan half-and-half. Stir only until a shaggy-looking dough forms. Turn the dough out onto a lightly floured surface and knead just enough to bring it together. With a rolling pin, gently roll the dough to a ¼-inch thickness. Fold the dough in half and repeat this step twice, for a total of three folds, then roll the dough into a ¾-inch round. Using a 2¼-inch floured biscuit cutter, punch out the biscuits using a straight downward motion rather than twisting. Place the biscuits on a parchment-lined baking sheet and bake 10–12 minutes, or until golden brown. Brush with the melted vegan butter and serve.

Makes 12 biscuits.

Cheddar Biscuits

This is an easy and adaptable drop biscuit, so there's no worry about overhandling. When I'm making a quick dinner and time is short, I mix up a batch of these biscuits and let them bake as I'm working on another dish or preparing a salad. They are as well received as if I had spent hours delicately shaping a croissant. You can experiment with the spices, based on what you are serving. They go especially well with Pasta with Bean Soup or Creamy Potato Soup (see chapter 6).

⅓ cup unsweetened soy milk
1 teaspoon apple cider vinegar
1¾ cups unbleached all-
   purpose flour
2 teaspoons baking powder
½ teaspoon garlic powder
½ teaspoon onion powder
1 teaspoon dried parsley

1 tablespoon sugar
½ teaspoon sea salt
½ cup grated vegan cheddar
½ stick vegan butter
2 tablespoons vegan egg
   powder mixed with ¾ cup
   very cold water, or ¾ cup
   Just Egg

Preheat oven to 375 degrees. Line a cookie sheet with parchment paper and set aside. Combine the soy milk and vinegar and allow it to thicken. In a large bowl, sift together the flour, baking powder, garlic powder, onion powder, parsley, sugar, and salt. Add the grated vegan cheddar and mix well. Add the vegan butter in small cubes and combine with the flour mixture using your hands or a pastry cutter until it resembles coarse meal. Mix the thickened soy milk with the vegan egg and stir into the flour mixture until just combined and a stiff dough forms. Using an ice cream scoop or large spoon, drop 6 spoonfuls of batter onto the cookie sheet. Bake for 30 minutes, until golden brown and a toothpick inserted in the center of each biscuit comes out clean.

Serves 6.

Half-Moon Dinner Rolls

This recipe uses the bread machine for mixing and rising. This reduces your workload and allows you to turn out an impressively shaped dinner roll with minimal effort. I choose these rolls for small gatherings or for weekday dinners if I need a couple of hours to chop and stir while the bread machine works its magic. I personally like the crescent moon shape, but feel free to indulge your creative spirit.

¾ cup plus 2 tablespoons unsweetened almond milk

2 cups unbleached all-purpose flour

½ cup whole wheat flour

2 teaspoons bread machine yeast

½ teaspoon sea salt

2 tablespoons sorghum syrup

1 tablespoon vegan butter

Place all the ingredients in the bread machine in the order listed and turn it to the rise setting. Line a baking sheet with parchment paper and set aside. When the cycle is complete, turn the dough out onto a lightly floured surface, divide it into 2 pieces, and roll each piece into a 12-inch circle. Cut each circle into 8 wedges and roll up each wedge, starting from the wide end. Place the rolls point side down on the baking sheet and curve the ends slightly to form a half-moon. Preheat oven to 375 degrees. Cover the rolls and let them rise in a warm place for about 30 minutes, or until doubled in size. Bake for 10–15 minutes, or until the tops are browned.

Serves 6–8.

Wheat Germ Dinner Rolls

I love the flavor of wheat germ. It not only tastes great but also ups the nutritional ante when added to baked goods or cereals. Wheat germ is a good source of vegetable protein, so you can say with confidence, "Yes, I'm vegan, and no, I'm not protein deficient." It also contains magnesium, zinc, thiamine, folate, potassium, phosphorus, and that caped antioxidant crusader vitamin E to fight off those pesky free radicals. And you can get all this healthy goodness from a humble dinner roll. So roll up your sleeves and get to work. And if you prefer a cape to an apron, no one needs to know.

2¼ teaspoons active dry yeast
¼ cup warm water
2 cups bread flour
½ cup whole wheat flour
¼ cup toasted wheat germ

¾ teaspoon sea salt
3 tablespoons vegan butter, melted
3 tablespoons sorghum syrup

Dissolve the yeast in warm water and set aside for 10 minutes. Combine both flours, wheat germ, and salt in a large bowl and whisk to combine. Add the melted vegan butter and sorghum syrup to the yeast mixture and stir to incorporate. Add the yeast mixture to the flour mixture. Turn the shaggy dough out onto a well-floured surface and knead for 10–15 minutes, adding more flour as necessary. Alternatively, place the dough in a stand mixer and use the dough hook to knead for approximately 8 minutes. Place the dough in a large buttered bowl, turning once to coat the top. Cover and let rise in a warm, draft-free place for 45 minutes, or until doubled in bulk. Punch the dough down and divide it into quarters. Divide each quarter into 4 balls and place the 16 balls in a greased 9-inch baking pan. Cover the dough and let it rise again for 45 minutes, or until doubled in size. Preheat oven to 375 degrees. Brush the tops of the rolls with melted vegan butter and bake for 15–20 minutes, or until golden brown. Serve warm.

Serves 6–8.

Pumpkin Bread

As soon as the first hint of autumn slices the Kentucky air, I open the windows and bake a batch of this bread. It's delicious right out of the oven but keeps for several days if tightly wrapped. I usually make a pot of chili the same day, and some pumpkin spice is the perfect end to a fall meal. This recipe makes 2 loaves, so you can share one with a friend or neighbor.

3 cups sugar
1 cup canola oil
1 15-ounce can pumpkin
    puree
½ cup applesauce
1 tablespoon egg replacer
    powder
3½ cups all-purpose flour

2 teaspoons baking soda
1 teaspoon baking powder
2 teaspoons salt
1 teaspoon nutmeg
1 teaspoon allspice
1 teaspoon cinnamon
½ teaspoon ground cloves
⅔ cup water

Preheat oven to 350 degrees. Oil and flour two 9- by 5-inch loaf pans and set aside. Mix the sugar and canola oil with an electric mixer at medium speed until well combined. Add the pumpkin, applesauce, and powdered egg replacer. Mix until smooth. Whisk together the flour, baking soda, baking powder, salt, and spices. With the electric mixer at low speed, add small portions of the flour mixture alternating with the water, combining well after each addition. Pour into the loaf pans and bake for 1 hour, or until a toothpick inserted in the center comes out clean. Cool on a wire rack for 15 minutes. Remove the bread from the pans and continue to cool until ready to serve.

Makes 2 loaves.

Vegetables and Sides

Vegetables and Sides

As I'm working through my list of side dishes to decide which ones to include in this chapter, gardens everywhere in Kentucky are beginning to color our tables with fresh strawberries, asparagus, and scallions. Farmer's markets beckon, encouraging us to grab something fresh and connect with the food's origins by meeting the folks who grew it. Colorful roadside stands are in abundance. In short, this is a dangerous time of year for me because I have never met a produce stand that didn't call my name.

I once tried to talk my way out of a ticket by proclaiming I absolutely could not have been speeding because there was a fruit market on my immediate left and I had never driven by one of those at sixty-five miles an hour. I stand by that claim, but I received both a ticket and an insurance rate hike that beg to differ.

In one of my previous jobs, I was a consultant at several nursing homes, and I often took my kids (who were home-schooled) along to play bingo and entertain the residents by serenading them with their fiddle and mandolin. Needless to say, they were thrilled with these jaunts. Especially memorable was a trip to Inez, Kentucky, which is about as far east as you can go in Kentucky without falling off the edge. On the way home, I spotted a combination video rental–pool hall–fruit stand wedged among so many aboveground pools and trampolines that the road could have been engineered by Doctor Seuss himself. When my head swiveled at the sight of a few paltry tomatoes on display, my kids said in unison, "Don't even think about it." Then they reminded me of the previous week's stop at a very sketchy music store that had one lone guitar but, oddly, what appeared to be a steady clientele. No produce was involved, but they were wary after that.

Naturally, there are endless possibilities when preparing a vegetable side-dish chapter in a plant-based cookbook, so I had some hard choices to make to narrow it down. The first few recipes are dishes that I often combine for a vegetable plate. A meal of three vegetable dishes, slaw, macaroni, and some crunchy cornbread is a year-round favorite at our house. You'll find everyday dishes along with traditional holiday fare that your nonvegan friends and relatives won't gawk at with a questioning eye. Get out your chopping board and enjoy the season's best!

Green Beans and New Potatoes

After my final year of high school, I entered a pageant at the county fair. One of the deep, philosophical questions posed to contestants was, "What is your favorite food?" In contrast to the popular choices of pizza, cheeseburgers, and ice cream, I announced that mine was green beans, and the audience burst into laughter. If my life was a movie, I suppose this would be called foreshadowing. I left without a ribbon but with my love of green beans firmly intact.

In my family, the white half-runner reigns supreme, and we look forward to the first "mess" of the season cooked with new potatoes and served with whatever other fresh vegetables are available. Throughout the summer months, there is usually a pot of green beans in the refrigerator ready to heat up for a quick dinner or a wholesome lunch paired with tomatoes, cucumbers, and onions.

2½ pounds green beans
1 package smoked tempeh
    bacon
2 tablespoons olive oil,
    divided
1 whole yellow onion

1 teaspoon dried savory
½ teaspoon liquid smoke
10 small red potatoes
Smoked sea salt and freshly
    ground black pepper to
    taste

Wash, string, and break the beans and set aside. Chop the tempeh bacon into small pieces. In a small nonstick skillet, heat 1 table-spoon olive oil and brown the tempeh bacon until crisp. Remove from the heat and allow to cool. In a large pot, combine the beans, onion, savory, liquid smoke, and 1 tablespoon olive oil. Cover with water (plus an extra inch for the later addition of the potatoes). Bring to a boil, reduce heat, and simmer for 30 minutes. Add the potatoes, return to a simmer, and cook loosely covered for 30–45 minutes, or until the potatoes are tender when pierced with a fork. Just before serving, season with salt and pepper and stir in the tempeh bacon.

Serves 8–10.

Skillet Corn

Like green beans and new potatoes, skillet corn epitomizes plant-based comfort food. I use fresh corn whenever possible, but because this is such regular fare at our house, I'm happy to use organic frozen yellow or white corn when need be. This dish is deceptively simple to make, and if you take it to a potluck, I promise you won't be queried for an ingredients list or be eating it as leftovers for the next three days.

4 cups corn, cut from about
    8 ears fresh corn, or 2
    16-ounce bags frozen corn
4 tablespoons vegan butter
½ cup water
1 tablespoon sugar

2 teaspoons salt
½ cup cold vegan
    half-and-half
2 tablespoons flour
Salt and freshly ground black
    pepper to taste

Melt the vegan butter in a large skillet, add water, sugar, and salt, and bring to a boil. Add the corn and cook, stirring occasionally, for 10–15 minutes. Dissolve the flour in the vegan half-and-half and drizzle into the corn mixture through a mesh sieve to remove any lumps. Stir until the mixture is thickened. Taste for seasoning. Serve immediately.

Serves 8.

Creamy Mashed Potatoes

This is a recipe that every cook wants in her wheelhouse. Both my grandmothers used an electric mixer to obtain that melt-in-your-mouth buttery taste and texture, but I'm a ricer convert. That's as close to Appalachian blasphemy as I get in this book. I believe the potato ricer is as essential as the cast-iron skillet, and it ensures that your mashed potatoes will be creamy. Another benefit of the ricer is that you can cook the potatoes with the skins on, saving time and avoiding the absorption of too much moisture.

4 pounds russet or gold
    potatoes, washed and
    scrubbed
1 tablespoon plus 2 teaspoons
    sea salt, divided
1 stick vegan butter at room
    temperature

½ cup vegan sour cream
½ cup vegan cream cheese,
    softened
1 cup warm unsweetened
    almond milk
Freshly ground black pepper

Place the potatoes in a large pot and cover with cold water plus 1 inch. Bring to a boil and add 1 tablespoon sea salt. Reduce the heat and simmer the potatoes for 30–35 minutes, or until tender when pierced with a fork. Drain the potatoes, rinse with cold water, then place them back in the pot over the warm burner (turned off) to dry the potatoes and keep them warm. Place the vegan butter in a large bowl and rice each potato into the bowl. Remove the potato skins in the ricer after each addition. Stir until the butter is fully incorporated into the potatoes. Combine the sour cream, cream cheese, and almond milk and stir into the potatoes with a large fork until smooth. Add 2 teaspoons sea salt and freshly ground black pepper to taste and serve immediately.

If desired, this recipe can be made a day ahead, covered with foil, and refrigerated. Before serving, bring the potatoes to room temperature and dot the top with vegan butter. Bake uncovered at 350 degrees until heated through.

Serves 8.

Macaroni and Cheese

Mac and cheese covers the bases for kids of all ages. It's a crowd pleaser but also a no-fuss dish that comes together with minimal effort. This version delivers lots of cheesy flavor. It can fly solo as a side dish or is perfectly amenable to the addition of diced tomatoes, broccoli, and seitan if you want a simple but delicious main dish to accompany a green salad and fresh bread. By substituting a different pasta and shaking up the seasonings, you have a jumping-off point for an endless variety of tasty one-dish meals.

8 ounces elbow macaroni

1 tablespoon sea salt

½ cup whole raw cashews

½ cup filtered water

1 cup no-chicken broth

7 ounces vegan cheddar

1 teaspoon Dijon mustard

¼ teaspoon paprika

2 tablespoons vegan butter

2 tablespoons all-purpose flour

Cook the macaroni according to package directions, adding the sea salt once the water starts to boil. Meanwhile, place the cashews in a high-speed blender and process until finely ground. Add the water and process an additional 1–2 minutes, or until smooth. Add the broth and process another 1–2 minutes. Cut the vegan cheddar into small blocks and add to the blender mixture. Process 2 minutes, or until thick and creamy. Add the Dijon and paprika to the blender and pulse to combine. Heat the vegan butter over low heat in a medium saucepan until melted. Whisk in the flour until no lumps remain. Add the cheddar mixture to the saucepan and increase the heat to medium. Cook and stir until thickened and just at the boiling point. Drain the cooked macaroni and return it to the pot. Stir the cheese sauce into the macaroni and serve immediately.

Serves 8.

Spiced Apples

In the fall, we love to go to Haney's Appledale Farm in Nancy, Kentucky. I grew up just down the road, and I later took my kids there to pick apples. Now the tradition continues with my young niece and nephew and my grandchildren. When we haul in that giant bag of apples, the first recipe in line is an apple crisp, but spiced apples are a close second. Tart apples cooked with butter, nutmeg, and cinnamon are a great accompaniment to a hearty breakfast of scrambled tofu and hash brown casserole or a dinner of fried chick'n. The Granny Smith is always a favorite cooking apple, but I like to use a mixture when the choices are abundant.

Be sure to taste the apples beforehand because each variety has its own flavor profile.

8 apples, peeled and sliced	½ teaspoon nutmeg
¼ cup vegan butter	Pinch sea salt
¼ cup water	¼ cup sorghum syrup
1 teaspoon cinnamon	1 tablespoon fresh lemon juice

In a medium saucepan, melt the vegan butter over low heat. Stir in the apples to coat, add the water, and bring to a simmer. Stir in the remaining ingredients and continue to simmer, stirring frequently, for 20 minutes, or until the apples are tender and glazed. Serve immediately or cover and store in the refrigerator for up to 2 days. Reheat before serving.

Serves 8.

Twice-Baked Potatoes

These tasty gems are my go-to potato for a cookout. They don't need much attention until the last minute (allowing you to focus on the grill, the marinade, and the like), yet they have a semi-fancy presentation. For busy cooks, this is an irresistible combination. I frequently pair them with marinated kebobs, green salad, and homemade rolls, but they are equally good with BBQ grilled chick'n and slaw.

8 large baking potatoes, scrubbed	¼ cup vegan sour cream
1 tablespoon olive oil	¼ teaspoon freshly ground black pepper
2 teaspoons sea salt, divided	1¼ cups grated vegan cheddar, divided
¼ cup vegan butter at room temperature	2 tablespoons chopped chives
½ cup warm unsweetened almond or oat milk	

Preheat oven to 450 degrees. Rub the potatoes with olive oil and 1 teaspoon sea salt. Place on a baking sheet and bake for 1 hour, or until tender when pierced with a fork. Allow the potatoes to cool until they can be handled. Make a small slice in the center of each potato and use a small spoon to carefully scrape the cooked potato into a large bowl, leaving the skins of the potatoes intact. Add the remaining 1 teaspoon sea salt and the vegan butter and stir to combine. Add the milk, vegan sour cream, black pepper, and 1 cup grated cheddar and mash with a handheld potato masher until blended but not perfectly smooth. Scoop the mixture back into the potato skins, top with the remaining ¼ cup vegan cheddar, and return to the oven until the cheese is melted and the potatoes are slightly browned. Top with chives and serve.

Serves 8.

Sweet Potato Casserole

I wasn't introduced to this dish until I was an adult. If it was on the table when I was growing up, I must have bypassed it for more green beans or one of my grandmother's desserts. The first time my friend Michelle brought this dish to a family dinner, I was smitten. I loved the deep caramel flavor and the crunchy nutty topping. I kindly requested the recipe, veganized it posthaste, and have been making it ever since.

CASSEROLE

2 cups cooked or canned sweet potatoes

1¼ cups brown sugar

2 tablespoons vegan egg powder

¾ cup very cold water

½ cup unsweetened almond milk

6 tablespoons vegan butter, melted

1 teaspoon pure vanilla extract

½ teaspoon cinnamon

½ teaspoon nutmeg

TOPPING

2 tablespoons unbleached all-purpose flour	½ cup pecans
½ cup brown sugar	6 tablespoons vegan butter, melted

Preheat oven to 350 degrees. In a large bowl, combine sweet potatoes and brown sugar. Whisk the vegan egg powder into the cold water and add to the potato mixture along with the almond milk, vegan butter, vanilla, cinnamon, and nutmeg. Stir until completely mixed. Transfer to a casserole dish and bake for 20 minutes. To make the topping, toss together the flour, brown sugar, pecans, and melted butter. Remove the casserole from the oven, sprinkle the pecan mixture evenly over the top, and bake for an additional 10 minutes. Serve immediately, or make a day ahead and reheat before serving.

Serves 8.

Glazed Baby Carrots

This recipe brings together two favorite Appalachian ingredients, sorghum and bourbon, to give the humble carrot its due. Often unfairly relegated to the raw vegetable and dip tray, carrots cook quickly, are nutritious, and add a nice pop of color to the table. I prefer to cut my own matchsticks from larger carrots, but baby carrots are a good choice if you're pressed for time or not in the mood for the extra work of peeling and chopping.

1 stick (½ cup) vegan butter	½ cup fresh orange juice
4 cups matchstick or baby carrots	6 tablespoons bourbon
1 teaspoon minced fresh ginger root or ⅛ teaspoon ground ginger	1 tablespoon chopped flat-leaf parsley
½ cup sorghum syrup	Sea salt and freshly ground black pepper

Melt the vegan butter in a large skillet over low heat. Add the carrots, increase heat to medium-low, and sauté, stirring occasionally, for 10 minutes. Add the ginger and sorghum. Simmer for 2 minutes. Remove from the heat and stir in the orange juice and bourbon. Return to the heat, cover, and simmer for 5–7 minutes, or until the carrots are tender when pierced with a fork. Uncover and simmer another 5–7 minutes, until the liquid is syrupy and the carrots are glazed. Season with salt and pepper. Serve immediately.

Serves 8.

Broccoli Casserole

This recipe was a tough one. Vegetarian broccoli casserole is no big deal, but vegan broccoli casserole was a challenge. I was unwilling to forgo this favorite dish, so I dove in, and I think you'll be pleased with the results. It may be a little more complicated than some recipes—after all, we're replacing those condensed soups with ingredients we can actually recognize—but it's well worth the effort. Plus, you can tell Aunt Betty that it's cholesterol free.

3 10-ounce packages frozen chopped broccoli, thawed and thoroughly drained
1 teaspoon celery seed
½ teaspoon paprika
¾ cup nutritional yeast
¼ cup pine nuts
2 teaspoons onion powder
1 teaspoon garlic powder
½ teaspoon salt
1 tablespoon dried parsley
1 teaspoon freshly ground black pepper

1 tablespoon tamari
1 cup no-chicken or vegetable broth
1 8-ounce block vegan cheddar, cut into cubes
2 teaspoons Dijon mustard
3 tablespoons vegan butter
¼ cup unbleached all-purpose flour
Crushed crackers for topping (Ritz happen to be vegan)
Sea salt and freshly ground black pepper to taste

Preheat oven to 350 degrees. Place the broccoli in a 13- by 9-inch casserole dish. Place the celery seed, paprika, nutritional yeast, pine nuts, onion powder, garlic powder, salt, parsley, and black pepper in a high-speed blender and process until ground to a powder. Add the tamari, broth, vegan cheddar, and Dijon mustard and blend on high speed until completely smooth. Melt the vegan butter in a medium saucepan over low heat. Add the flour to the butter and stir until incorporated and lump free. Add the blender mixture to the saucepan and increase the heat to medium-low. Continue stirring until the mixture boils and thickens. Pour the sauce over the broccoli, sprinkle with crushed crackers, and bake 35–40 minutes, until browned and bubbly. Taste for seasoning and serve immediately.

Serves 8.

Cheese Grits

My paternal grandfather loved to load a random assortment of his seven grandkids into a van, along with his wife Elva, and drive sixteen hours to Disney World. Why he willingly subjected himself to this annual trip to Florida remains a family mystery. My sister and I would fight incessantly over my routine violations of a boundary line that was visible only to her, while the boy cousins joined in some rousing versions of very inappropriate AC/DC songs. My grandfather just drove the van and hummed very loudly.

One stopping point was always Macon, Georgia, to visit my aunt Marie's mom, Mrs. Coleman. About an hour before we arrived, my grandfather would begin to talk ad nauseam about her delicious grits. My grandmother also made grits and was a bit prideful and competitive when it came to her cooking skills. She never said much, but her lips would grow thinner and thinner as he chattered. I'm sure he loved the grits, but he also really liked to aggravate Elva.

We always arrived at bedtime, but the next morning Mrs. Coleman would send us on our way with a huge breakfast that included her legendary grits. This recipe for cheese grits is smoky and garlicky and is a perfect accompaniment to barbecued seitan or chick'n, as well as breakfast. I think my grandfather would be pleased.

4 cups water	½ teaspoon liquid smoke
¼ cup vegan butter	1½ teaspoons smoked sea salt
2 tablespoons chopped garlic	1 teaspoon Creole seasoning
½ teaspoon freshly ground	1 cup white corn grits
black pepper	1 cup shredded vegan cheese

In a medium pot, combine the water, vegan butter, garlic, black pepper, liquid smoke, sea salt, and Creole seasoning and bring to a boil. Slowly whisk in the grits and reduce the heat to low. Continue to cook, stirring constantly, for 10 minutes, or until thick and creamy. Remove from the heat and stir in the shredded vegan cheese. Let the grits stand until the cheese is fully melted. Stir and serve.

Serves 6–8.

Scalloped Cabbage

Once summer is in full swing, Kentucky gardens produce cabbage—and lots of it. I'm a heavy indulger when it comes to cruciferous vegetables, and I encourage others to join in. This recipe is simple to make and will please those folks who like a little creaminess to accompany their healthy vegetables.

1 small head cabbage, roughly	½ cup water
chopped	½ stick vegan butter
1 tablespoon sugar	2 tablespoons unbleached all-
3 cups vegetable or	purpose flour
no-chicken broth, divided	4 ounces vegan parmesan
½ cup cashews	

Preheat oven to 350 degrees. Toss the chopped cabbage with the sugar and place in a small casserole dish. Pour in enough of the broth to cover the cabbage. Cover with aluminum foil and bake for 30 minutes. Place the remaining broth, cashews, water, vegan butter, and flour in a high-speed blender and process until completely smooth. Pour the mixture over the cabbage and re-cover with foil. Bake for 15 minutes, remove the foil, and top with the vegan parmesan. Place the casserole back in the oven and bake uncovered for 15 minutes. Allow to sit for 10 minutes before serving.

Serves 8–10.

Okra, Corn, and Tomatoes

This popular local dish is both healthy and colorful, and Kelly's Market in Richmond, Kentucky, never lets me down with its beautiful produce. Unfortunately, although this dish is widely available when dining out, most restaurant versions include some type of animal product. Luckily, this vegan recipe is quick and easy to prepare. If you have leftovers, stir them into some heated cheese sauce to make a delicious dip for tortilla chips.

2 tablespoons olive oil
2 tablespoons vegan butter
1 small onion, diced
3 tomatoes, seeded and
    chopped
3 cups fresh corn
2 cups fresh okra, sliced

1 teaspoon liquid smoke
¾ teaspoon salt
½ teaspoon freshly ground
    black pepper
½ teaspoon Creole seasoning
¼ teaspoon dried thyme

Add the olive oil and vegan butter to a large skillet over medium-low heat and allow the butter to melt. Add the onion to the skillet, turn the heat to medium, and sauté the onion for 5 minutes, until translucent. Add the tomatoes, corn, and okra and cook for an additional 10 minutes, stirring occasionally. Add the liquid smoke, salt, pepper, Creole seasoning, and thyme and cook for another 5–10 minutes, until the vegetables are cooked through. Serve hot.

Serves 4–6.

Desserts

10

Desserts

R ecently, my son Cody snapped a photo of a bowl of Sunkist raisin boxes and sent it to his brother along with a tongue-in-cheek text that read, "Found some of our childhood candy bars." Before the accompanying photo came through, Jake replied, "What!? You got candy bars?" It's true that I encouraged healthy eating, but their memories fail them if they think they were denied their fair share of sweets.

The love of a beautiful dessert is universal, whether it's a frosted layer cake or a warm chocolate chip cookie with tongue-tingling flakes of sea salt. A visually pleasing touch of sweetness at the end of a meal is welcomed by all. My maternal grand-mother frequently cautioned me, "You can catch more flies with sugar than vinegar," and I see the parallel here (although I do wonder why this was such an oft-repeated phrase during my childhood).

I think of vegan desserts as a gateway food. Initially, some-one's plant-averse mind-set may be toppled by a fancy vegan cupcake with a creamy filling. Next, they may be willing to try some vegan mashed potatoes and gravy. Suddenly, they realize that not every plant-based meal comes on a bed of barley with a topping of kale, beets, and tofu. Personally, I adore each of those earthy ingredients, but I also embrace the theory that there is a plant-based menu for every palate.

This chapter includes recipes for every skill level. You can't go wrong with basics like oatmeal cookies or no-bake cookies. But if you want to try something a bit more challenging, dive into the triple-layer Italian cream cake or the chocolate pie with a beautiful aquafaba meringue. Just remember that veganism rules, and your sweet tooth need not compromise.

Fresh Peach Crisp

I once took a cruise to the Virgin Islands. Only moments after waving bon voyage to the shores of San Juan, a group I called the "Georgia Peaches" made their presence known. Despite the immense dimensions of the ship, I could not escape this four-some. The pool, the midnight buffet, the lido deck—everywhere I went, there they were. They were lovely human specimens whose long locks shone, despite the sea air that crimped mine into a frizzy halo; they had perfect toothy smiles, adorable southern accents, and stunning wardrobes. Yet in all their glory, they simply could not find contentment unless every eye was trained on them—and most of them already were. With only a trace of sour grapes, I can say that my definition of attention-getting behavior was redefined that week at sea. The memory of the Georgia Peaches always comes to mind whenever I prepare this flavorful crisp. This dessert is sure to get plenty of attention, with no hair flipping, thong bikini, or hyena-like laughter required.

3 pounds peaches, peeled and sliced
⅓ cup sugar
Juice and zest of 1 small lemon
⅔ cup plus 2 tablespoons whole wheat pastry flour, divided
½ cup vegan butter at room temperature
¾ cup brown sugar
½ cup rolled oats
½ cup chopped pecans or walnuts
¼ teaspoon salt
¼ teaspoon allspice
¼ teaspoon cardamom
½ teaspoon ground cinnamon

Preheat oven to 350 degrees. Toss the peaches with the sugar, lemon juice, lemon zest, and 2 tablespoons flour and pour into a 2-inch-high baking dish or oiled cast-iron skillet. Combine the vegan butter, ⅔ cup flour, brown sugar, oats, nuts, salt, allspice, cardamom, and cinnamon and blend with the paddle attachment of an electric mixer at low speed. Alternatively, combine the ingredients with your hands, ensuring that every piece is coated and the mixture is coarse and crumbly. Sprinkle over the top of the peaches and bake for 25–30 minutes, until browned and bubbly around the edges. Serve with vegan ice cream or whipped topping.

Serves 8.

Chocolate Cream Pie

My paternal grandmother, Elva, was and will forever be the queen of pie making. No matter the flavor or the filling involved, each pie was a beautiful creation. Her high and fluffy meringues, browned to perfection, were as lovely to behold as they were to eat. Even more impressive was the speed at which she prepared them for our family's weekend restaurant business. It's no easy feat to turn out a dozen assorted pies from your home kitchen by 10:00 a.m. on a Saturday morning with a gaggle of grandkids itching to "assist." She was a tiny whirlwind, and watching her twirl each pie to crimp the crust with a fork and then deftly stack them in the oven was amazing. Whenever I prepare a cream pie, I offer up thanks for all those days I spent in her kitchen—and for the amazing discovery of aquafaba, which allows me to replicate a vegan version of meringue for those delicious recipes, albeit at a much slower pace. This recipe uses vegan semisweet chocolate chips and cocoa powder for a deep and satisfying chocolate flavor. Here's to Elva!

1 blind-baked pie crust at
     room temperature
2 tablespoons vegan butter
1½ cups vegan semisweet
     chocolate chips
1 teaspoon vanilla extract
1 teaspoon chocolate extract

1 cup sugar
¼ cup cornstarch
3 tablespoons unsweetened
     cocoa powder
¼ teaspoon salt
1 cup vegan sour cream

½ cup Just Egg or prepared   ⅓ cup aquafaba
   vegan egg replacer   ⅓ cup sugar
2 cups oat milk   ¼ teaspoon cream of tartar

For the pie crust, make half the recipe at the end of this chapter (this pie uses only a bottom crust). To blind-bake the crust, preheat the oven to 350 degrees. Prick the bottom of the crust all over with the tines of a fork. Place a sheet of parchment paper over the crust and fill with either pie weights or dried beans. Bake for 30 minutes, or until the pastry starts to brown around the edges. Remove the parchment and weights and continue baking for 10–20 minutes, until golden brown. Cool completely on a wire rack before filling.

To make the filling, place the vegan butter, chocolate chips, vanilla extract, and chocolate extract in a large bowl and set aside. In a large saucepan, whisk together the sugar, cornstarch, cocoa powder, and salt. Blend the vegan sour cream, Just Egg, and oat milk together and pour over the saucepan mixture, stirring until well combined. Bring to a boil over medium-low heat, stirring constantly. Continue to stir and boil for 1 minute. Remove from the heat and pour over the chocolate chips mixture. Let it stand for 3 minutes, then whisk until smooth. Pour into the prepared pie crust, cover with plastic wrap, and chill for at least 4 hours or overnight.

To make the meringue, in a mixer bowl, combine the aquafaba, sugar, and cream of tartar and mix at low speed for 2 minutes. Turn the speed to medium and beat for 2 minutes. Increase the speed to high and continue to beat for 4–6 minutes, until fluffy and stiff peaks form. Spread the meringue evenly over the pie filling and use a butane torch to brown the meringue. Alternatively, broil on low in the oven, monitoring closely, until the top is browned.

Serves 7.

Italian Cream Cake

The first time my grandmother made this cake for a holiday gathering, I thought it was the best cake I had ever eaten. After that, I frequently ordered it when dining out, but the restaurant versions never measured up. Despite a beautiful presentation, they were always too dry or flavorless. And although we all appreciate pretty packaging, everyone knows that it's what's inside that counts. So veganizing this treasured recipe was a bit like my personal ascent of Meru. Again, aquafaba comes to the rescue. Tap into your creative spirit to swirl or pipe the icing and sprinkle the nuts and coconut liberally over the top. It's going to be bellissimo!

CAKE

1 cup aquafaba
2 cups sugar
1 tablespoon lemon juice
½ cup canola oil
½ cup melted vegan shortening
¼ cup applesauce
1 tablespoon vanilla extract

3 cups unbleached all-purpose flour
2 tablespoons baking powder
1½ teaspoons sea salt
1 cup chopped pecans, plus 2 tablespoons for garnish
1 cup sweetened coconut, plus 2 tablespoons for garnish

FROSTING

½ stick vegan butter
8 ounces vegan cream cheese

1 pound powdered sugar
1 teaspoon vanilla extract

Preheat oven to 350 degrees. Oil and flour three 9-inch cake pans, then line the bottom of each pan with parchment paper. To make the cake, place the aquafaba in a bowl and beat with an electric mixer at high speed until light and fluffy, about 2 minutes. Slowly add the sugar while continuing to beat at high speed for about

5 minutes, until stiff peaks start to form. Combine the lemon juice, canola oil, shortening, applesauce, and vanilla in a small bowl. Add this mixture to the aquafaba mixture, beating just until incorporated. Sift together the flour, baking powder, and salt. Using a spatula, fold the dry ingredients into the wet mixture until just combined. Do not overmix. Fold in 1 cup pecans and 1 cup coconut. Divide the batter evenly among the 3 cake pans and bake for 30–35 minutes, or until a cake tester inserted in the center comes out clean. I recommend testing at about 30 minutes. Allow the cakes to cool on a wire rack for 20 minutes before removing from the pans; then place on the rack to cool completely. Prepare the frosting by creaming together the vegan butter and cream cheese for 2 minutes. Gradually add the sugar, mixing well after each addition. Stir in the vanilla and beat at high speed for 5 minutes. Frost the top of each layer as you stack them to assemble the cake. Frost the sides of the cake and sprinkle the frosted top with the remaining pecans and coconut.

Serves 8–10.

Peanut Butter Chocolate Chip Blondies

This is my whip-up-in-a-hurry crowd pleaser. It's easy to throw together, and the peanut butter and chocolate combination is always well received. I top it with vegan vanilla ice cream and a swirl of chocolate syrup. When it comes to deliciousness versus time spent, the ratio is in your favor here. This dessert also travels well (without toppings), so it's a great choice when you're asked to bring the last course to a cookout or a picnic. (I know I bring up picnics a lot, but that's because I love them.)

½ cup creamy peanut butter
4 tablespoons vegan butter
1 cup brown sugar
1 teaspoon vanilla extract

2 tablespoons vegan egg powder mixed with ½ cup very cold water
⅔ cup unbleached all-purpose flour

1 teaspoon baking soda

¼ teaspoon sea salt

½ cup vegan semisweet
  chocolate chips

½ cup chopped salted
  peanuts, divided

Preheat oven to 350 degrees. Oil and flour an 8-inch square baking pan. Line the bottom of the pan with parchment paper. Combine the peanut butter, vegan butter, brown sugar, and vanilla and mix with an electric mixer at medium speed until well combined. Add the vegan egg mixture and mix at high speed until light and fluffy. Whisk together the flour, baking soda, and salt and stir into the peanut butter mixture. Fold in the chocolate chips and ¼ cup peanuts. Pour the batter into the prepared pan and smooth to ensure an even distribution. Top with the remaining ¼ cup peanuts. Bake for 25–30 minutes, until the top looks dry and a cake tester inserted in the center comes out clean. Cool slightly before serving.

Serves 6–8.

Chocolate No-Bake Cookies

In sixth grade, my 4-H demonstration project was how to make no-bake cookies. With my sparkly posters, kitchen savvy, and much help from my teacher Lucy Flannery, I made it all the way to the state competition. I didn't win first place, but for the record, it wasn't because someone else made better cookies. I was defeated by a twelve-year-old tire-changer with superior communication skills. I make these cookies frequently because they are quick, easy, and loved by people of all ages. This is my original sixth-grade recipe with vegan substitutions for the milk and butter. As they say, if it ain't broke . . .

1 stick vegan butter

⅓ cup cocoa

2 cups sugar

½ cup unsweetened soy milk

3 cups quick-cooking oats

½ cup creamy peanut butter

¼ teaspoon sea salt

1½ teaspoons vanilla extract

Grease a 9-inch square baking pan and set aside. In a saucepan over medium heat, melt the vegan butter and stir in the cocoa, sugar, and soy milk. Stir the mixture constantly and bring it to a boil. Boil for 1 minute (you might want to set a timer). Remove from the heat and stir in the oats, peanut butter, salt, and vanilla. Pour into the prepared pan and cool on a wire rack until set. Slice into squares to serve.

Makes 16 cookies.

Chocolate Chip Cookies

What dessert is nearer and dearer to our hearts than the chocolate chip cookie? I have no idea how many dozens I have made over the years, but I'm guessing that if they were strung together, I could have aided the brilliant Greek librarian Eratosthenes in his calculations of the earth's circumference. This recipe delivers everything you could want from this steadfast lunchbox companion. The cookies are soft and chewy, brown nicely, and have a little extra salt to enhance the chocolate flavor. You'll want to eat one while it's warm and then a few more. That's okay. This recipe makes 2 dozen large or 3 dozen small cookies, so nobody will mind.

¾ cup sugar
¾ cup brown sugar
1 cup vegan butter, softened
1 tablespoon vanilla extract
⅓ cup applesauce
1 tablespoon vegan egg
   replacer powder
2¼ cups unbleached all-
   purpose flour

1 teaspoon baking soda
1 teaspoon salt
1 12-ounce bag vegan
   semisweet chocolate chips
½ cup old-fashioned rolled
   oats
½ cup chopped pecans or
   walnuts (optional)
Sea salt for garnish (optional)

Preheat oven to 350 degrees. Line a baking sheet with parchment paper and set aside. With an electric mixer, cream together both sugars and the vegan butter. Add the vanilla, applesauce, and vegan egg replacer. Beat at medium-high speed until fluffy and creamy, 2–3 minutes. Sift together the flour, baking soda, and salt and add to the butter mixture. Mix at low speed until fully incorporated. Fold in the chocolate chips, oats, and nuts. Drop by rounded tablespoons onto the baking sheet. Bake for 12–15 minutes, or until golden brown. Cool on a wire rack. Garnish with flaky sea salt if desired.

Makes 24 large or 36 small cookies.

Oatmeal Cookies

Nothing says comfort like a chewy oatmeal cookie. When life's undertow gets too strong, I put on some Cat Stevens (aka Yusuf) and bake a batch of these cookies. I use currants because I like their small size and texture, but raisins also work. So crank up "Peace Train," let the fresh-baked smell permeate the kitchen, and all will be right with the world (at least temporarily).

1 cup unbleached all-purpose flour	¼ cup applesauce
¼ teaspoon baking powder	1 tablespoon vegan egg replacer powder
¼ teaspoon baking soda	1 teaspoon vanilla extract
½ teaspoon cinnamon	1½ cups rolled oats
½ teaspoon salt	½ cup currants
½ cup vegan butter	½ cup chopped walnuts or pecans
⅔ cup light brown sugar	
⅓ cup sugar	

Preheat oven to 350 degrees. In a mixing bowl, whisk together the flour, baking powder, baking soda, cinnamon, and salt and set aside. With an electric mixer, cream the vegan butter until light and fluffy. Add both sugars and beat for 2 minutes. Add the applesauce and vegan egg replacer and continue mixing until fully combined and fluffy. Add the vanilla and then stir in the flour mixture. Add the oats, currants, and nuts. Stir until the mixture is uniform. Drop by tablespoons on a parchment-lined baking sheet and bake for 12 minutes, or until golden brown. Oven temperatures vary, so start checking for doneness after 10 minutes.

Makes 24 cookies.

Half-Moon Pies

I spent much of my youth horseback riding on the wooded trails of Estill County. Both the scenic beauty and the camaraderie of my horse-loving friends account for some of my fondest childhood memories. The barn where I kept my horse, Cinder, sat on property owned by the Arvin family, and it was graced with a large, gnarled apple tree. Cinder and I would frequently park underneath it and pluck one (or several) apples from the branches for an afternoon snack. However, the best thing about that tree was the apple pies made every fall by Elsie, matriarch of the Arvin family. Sweet, delicate, and shaped like half-moons, they were delicious whether eaten warm and freshly prepared or cold after a long day of riding. Elsie was under no obligation to feed the steady stream of young riders who clustered around her home every day, yet she often did. Her generosity helped me understand that you can make someone's day better simply by opening your home and your kitchen. When I make my annual trip to Haney's Appledale Farm, I grab some dried apples and make a batch of these pies to share and pay it forward.

2¼ cups unbleached all-purpose flour, plus more for dusting the kneading surface

1¼ teaspoons sea salt, divided

½ teaspoon baking powder

1 cup oat milk, warmed to just below boiling

½ cup vegan shortening, chilled and cut into small pieces

2 cups dried apples

2 cups water

2 tablespoons vegan butter

½ cup sorghum syrup

¾ teaspoon ground cinnamon

Pinch ground mace

Peanut oil for frying

Powdered sugar

In a medium bowl, whisk together the flour, 1 teaspoon sea salt, and baking powder. In a large mixing bowl, combine the warm oat milk with the chilled shortening and stir until the pieces of shortening are pea sized. Add the flour mixture to the milk and stir with a fork until a soft dough forms. Roll the dough into a ball and knead on a lightly floured surface until smooth. Roll the dough into a log shape, cover in plastic wrap, and chill for at least 2 hours. While the dough is chilling, combine the dried apples with the water and vegan butter in a medium saucepan. Bring the mixture to a boil; then cover and cook over low heat for 40–45 minutes, stirring occasionally and adding more water if necessary, until the apples soften and all the liquid has been absorbed. Remove from the heat and stir in the sorghum, cinnamon, mace, and remaining ¼ teaspoon salt. Mash with a potato masher to combine. Set aside to cool to room temperature.

Once the apples are cool, divide the dough into 12 equal balls and roll each into a 6-inch circle on a floured surface. You may want to keep the dough chilled as you work. Place 2 tablespoons apple filling on the bottom half of each dough round. Fold the dough over into a half-moon shape and use a dampened fork to crimp the edges to prevent leakage of the filling. Heat ½ inch peanut oil in a heavy skillet over medium-high heat. Working in batches to prevent overcrowding, fry the pies for about 5 minutes on each side, until golden brown. Remove from the skillet and cool slightly on a wire rack. Dust with powdered sugar and serve warm or at room temperature.

Makes 12 pies.

Strawberry Shortcake

I herald spring with this favorite dessert. You can't go wrong with fresh strawberries. In the past, I was never completely satisfied with the cake portion of this recipe, based on the memory of my grandmother's kitchen wizardry. Then, a couple of years ago, I added vegan egg to the dough, and now my shortcake meets Elva's light and fluffy standard. Bring on the whipped cream and dig in!

FILLING

1 quart fresh strawberries
¼ cup sugar

1 teaspoon lemon zest

SHORTCAKE

⅔ cup soy milk, plus additional to brush on cake tops
1 teaspoon apple cider vinegar
2¼ cups all-purpose flour
½ cup plus 1 tablespoon sugar, divided
1½ teaspoons baking powder
¾ teaspoon baking soda
¼ teaspoon salt
6 tablespoons vegan butter, chilled

1 tablespoon vegan egg powder mixed with ¼ cup very cold water
1 teaspoon pure vanilla extract
⅛ teaspoon almond extract
Whipped cream (see recipe at the end of this chapter)
Additional strawberries for garnish

To make the filling, place strawberries, sugar, and lemon zest in a large bowl and toss to combine. Use the back of a wooden spoon to gently press the berries into the sugar. Allow to sit at room temperature for 1 hour until a light syrup forms. Chill until ready to serve.

Preheat oven to 425 degrees. To make the shortcake, whisk together the soy milk and vinegar and set aside to thicken. In a food processor, briefly pulse the flour, ½ cup sugar, baking powder, baking soda, and salt to combine. Add the vegan butter and pulse until only pea-sized pieces remain. Stir the vegan egg mixture into the soy milk along with the vanilla and almond extracts. Drizzle over the flour mixture and pulse 2–3 times to barely incorporate. Turn the dough onto a lightly floured sheet of wax paper and gently fold it on top of itself 3 times. Use an ice cream scoop to make 6 balls of dough and place them on a parchment-lined baking sheet. Do not flatten the dough. Cover and chill for 20 minutes. Brush the tops of the dough balls with additional soy milk and sprinkle with the remaining 1 tablespoon sugar. Bake for 25 minutes, or until golden brown. Cool slightly.

To assemble, split the shortcakes using a serrated knife. Divide the strawberries among the 6 shortcake bottoms. Place whipped cream on top of the berries and cover with the shortcake tops. Garnish with a few additional berries and more whipped cream.

Makes 6 shortcakes.

Pineapple Upside-Down Cake

Want to make good use of your cast-iron skillet? Whip up this quick and easy cake. Rumor has it that Fannie Farmer made this dessert famous, but this veganized version lacks nothing. As a kid, I was always tempted to pluck those colorful maraschino cherries out of the centers of the pineapple rings. As an adult, I can do just that. I like to serve this dessert as the finale to traditional meals such as vegetable plates or fried chick'n and mashed potatoes.

1 20-ounce can pineapple rings
12 tablespoons vegan butter, divided
⅔ cup firmly packed brown sugar
Maraschino cherries
1½ cups unbleached all-purpose flour
½ cup sugar

2 teaspoons baking powder
½ teaspoon sea salt
½ cup soy milk
1 tablespoon vegan egg replacer powder mixed with ¼ cup very cold water, or ¼ cup Just Egg
1 teaspoon lemon juice
1 teaspoon vanilla extract
½ teaspoon lemon zest

Preheat oven to 400 degrees. Drain the pineapple, setting aside 2 tablespoons of the liquid. Melt 4 tablespoons vegan butter in a 10-inch cast-iron skillet. Stir in the brown sugar until blended.

Remove from the heat and add the reserved pineapple juice. Arrange the pineapple rings in the skillet with the sugar mixture and place a maraschino cherry in the center of each one. In a bowl, whisk together the flour, sugar, baking powder, and salt and set aside. Melt the remaining 8 tablespoons vegan butter in a saucepan, remove from the heat, and stir in the soy milk, vegan egg mixture, lemon juice, vanilla, and lemon zest. Add the flour mixture to the liquid ingredients and mix until smooth. Pour the batter over the pineapple in the skillet and spread evenly. Place the skillet in the oven and bake for 35–40 minutes, or until a toothpick inserted in the center comes out clean. Cool on a wire rack for 5–10 minutes and invert onto a serving dish. Serve warm.

Serves 8.

Bourbon Pecan Pie

This is a rich and satisfying vegan twist on a classic Kentucky dessert. I like to use the buttery pie crust recipe included in this chapter, but a prebaked crust works just as well. Serve this pie warm, topped with vegan whipped cream or ice cream, and a steaming cup of Kahlua and coffee.

1 blind-baked 9-inch pie crust (see Pie Crust recipe near the end of this chapter for blind-baking instructions)
½ cup vegan butter, melted
½ cup sugar
½ cup dark corn syrup
½ cup Just Egg
2 tablespoons bourbon

1 teaspoon vanilla extract
¼ teaspoon sea salt
1 cup chopped pecans
1 cup vegan semisweet chocolate chips
½ cup pecan halves
1 tablespoon vegan cream (optional)

Preheat oven to 375 degrees. In a medium bowl, combine the vegan butter, sugar, corn syrup, Just Egg, bourbon, vanilla, and salt. Stir until fully mixed. Add the chopped pecans and chocolate chips and mix well. Pour the mixture into the prepared crust.

Arrange the pecan halves on top of the filling. Brush the pie edges with vegan cream. Bake for 40 minutes, or until the center is set and the crust is golden brown. Cool completely and serve with vegan ice cream or whipped cream.

Serves 7.

Carrot Cake

Everyone needs a sheet cake that is quick, delicious, and easy to transport to family gatherings, potlucks, and picnics. This is that cake. It's moist and yummy, with lots of nutritious ingredients and minimal cleanup. Every time I make it, I immediately want to make it again.

CAKE

2 cups unbleached all-purpose flour

2 teaspoons baking powder

1 teaspoon baking soda

2 teaspoons cinnamon

½ teaspoon allspice

1 teaspoon salt

¾ cup canola or grapeseed oil

1½ cups sugar

½ cup unsweetened applesauce

1 tablespoon egg replacer powder

2 teaspoons pure vanilla extract

1 cup finely chopped carrots

½ cup crushed pineapple, drained

1 cup chopped walnuts

1 cup shredded coconut

ICING

½ stick vegan butter

8 ounces vegan cream cheese

1 pound powdered sugar

1 teaspoon pure vanilla extract

Preheat oven to 350 degrees. Oil and flour a 13- by 9-inch baking pan. To make the cake, whisk together the flour, baking powder, baking soda, cinnamon, allspice, and salt and set aside. Cream the oil and sugar with an electric mixer at medium speed for about 2 minutes, or until well blended. Add the applesauce, egg replacer powder, and vanilla and continue beating until the mixture is smooth. Reduce the mixer speed to low and gradually add the flour mixture, beating until just combined. Fold in the carrots, pineapple, walnuts, and coconut. Spread the batter evenly in the prepared pan and bake for 45–60 minutes, until the top is golden brown and a toothpick or cake tester inserted in the center comes out clean. Cool on a wire rack. Prepare the icing by whipping together the vegan butter and cream cheese with an electric mixer at high speed until completely blended. Add the sugar a little at a time, blending well after each addition. Add the vanilla and mix for an additional 5 minutes. Spread evenly over the cooled cake and serve.

Serves 12.

Oreo Truffles

I, of course, was not the genius who came up with the Oreo truffle. I assume that honor belongs to the Kraft kitchen staff who asked themselves, "How else can we consume these chocolate vegan gems?" This veganized version is a crowd pleaser. I make them for every holiday gathering along with some chocolate-covered strawberries to make my dessert tray look beautiful.

36 Oreos, finely crushed (set aside ¼ cup crumbs for topping)

8 ounces vegan cream cheese, softened

16 ounces vegan semisweet chocolate chips, melted

Combine the crushed Oreos and vegan cream cheese either in a food processor or with an electric mixer at low speed. Shape into 48 (1-inch) balls and place on a rimmed baking sheet lined with wax paper. Freeze for 10 minutes. Dip the truffles in the melted chocolate chips in batches, using two forks to roll the truffles to ensure an even coating of chocolate. Remove the truffles with the forks and allow the excess chocolate to drip back into the bowl. Place the truffles back on the baking sheet and sprinkle with the reserved cookie crumbs. Let stand until firm. Serve immediately or store tightly covered in the refrigerator for up to 3 days.

Makes 48 truffles.

Chocolate Icebox Cake with Strawberry Sauce

Kentucky summers can be hot and humid. On days when you walk outdoors and can actually feel the air sitting on your skin, you know it's time for some icebox cake. This one is cool, rich, chocolaty deliciousness. I once had a leftover slice in my fridge that I couldn't stop thinking about, so I called home and had someone bring it to me at work. (I was worried that, as is often the case in my house, it wouldn't be there when I got home.) It does require some planning, since the chill time is 12 hours. However, you won't find a more perfect or visually pleasing end to a summer cookout or a long day at work. If you can't find plain vegan chocolate wafers, scrape the cream filling off Oreos and use them. We do what we have to do.

2 pints vegan sour cream
1 cup powdered sugar
1½ teaspoons vanilla extract
⅛ teaspoon salt
42 vegan chocolate wafers

1 pound strawberries, rinsed, hulled, and sliced
⅓ cup granulated sugar
1 tablespoon fresh lemon juice

Line a 9- by 5-inch loaf pan with plastic wrap. Place one sheet vertically and one horizontally, leaving a few inches hanging over the sides. In a medium bowl, whisk together the vegan sour cream, powdered sugar, vanilla, and salt until well combined and smooth. Arrange a layer of wafers on the bottom of the pan, keeping the layer as level as possible. Spread with 1 cup of the sour cream mixture. Repeat with 2 more layers of wafers and sour cream, ending with the sour cream mixture. Cover with plastic wrap and refrigerate for at least 12 hours. In a medium saucepan, combine the strawberries, granulated sugar, and lemon juice. Bring the mixture to a boil, stirring frequently. Reduce the heat and simmer for 20–25 minutes, stirring occasionally, until the sauce thickens. Remove from the heat and cool to room temperature before refrigerating. To serve, carefully lift the chilled icebox cake from the pan using the overhanging plastic wrap. Flip the cake onto a cutting board with the wafer side up and gently peel away the wrap. Spoon a couple of tablespoons of strawberry sauce on each serving plate. Using a sharp serrated knife, slice the cake into 10 portions. Arrange the slices on the serving plates and top with additional strawberry sauce if desired.

Serves 10.

Pie Crust

Pie crusts come in many varieties, including the ever-popular premade ones. Conveniently, some of them are vegan—just read the labels carefully. I prefer this light and buttery crust for most of my recipes. I recommend using a food processor, but if that's not an option, a pastry cutter will work.

2½ cups unbleached all-purpose flour

1 teaspoon sea salt

1 teaspoon sugar

1 cup vegan butter, diced into small pieces and chilled

¼–½ cup ice water

In the food processor, pulse together the flour, salt, and sugar. Add the diced vegan butter and pulse 8–10 times, until the mixture resembles coarse meal. With the machine running, slowly drizzle in ice water just until the dough holds together. Be careful not to overprocess. Divide the dough into 2 equal balls, place each on a sheet of wax paper, and flatten into discs. Make sure the dough is completely covered in the wax paper and chill in the refrigerator for at least 1 hour. On a lightly floured surface, roll each disc out into an 11-inch round. Place one in a 9-inch pie plate and fold under, trim, and crimp as desired. Use the second for the top crust.

To blind-bake the crust, preheat the oven to 350 degrees. Prick the bottom of the crust with the tines of a fork and place in the freezer for 15 minutes. Line the crust with parchment paper and fill with pie weights or dried beans. Bake for 20 minutes. Remove weights and parchment and return to the oven for an additional 5 minutes. Cool to room temperature before using in a recipe.

Makes two 9-inch pie crusts.

Fluffy Whipped Cream

This sweet, light topping is so wonderful you'll be tempted to eat giant spoonfuls before it even reaches your dessert. Don't say I didn't warn you. It keeps in the fridge for up to a week if covered tightly, so it's easy to make ahead of time.

½ cup cashews

1½ cups filtered water

1 cup refined coconut oil, melted

¼ cup sugar

2 teaspoons vanilla extract

Place the cashews and water in a high-speed blender and process until completely smooth. Add the coconut oil, sugar, and vanilla. Process for another 30 seconds, or until the mixture appears emulsified. Refrigerate for at least 6 hours, then beat with an electric mixer at high speed until stiff peaks start to form. Be careful not to overmix. Store covered in the refrigerator until ready to serve.

Serves 8–10.

Sauces, Gravies, Dressings, and Jam

11

Sauces, Gravies, Dressings, and Jam

This chapter is all about the backbone of vegan cooking: the marinades, dressings, sauces, and spreads that make our favorite recipes special. In this respect, science is our friend. When I'm developing new recipes, the recent surge in food science information makes my job easier. Understanding the amino acid profile or pH of a traditional dish can guide the selection of plant-based alternatives. Our current understanding of nutrition means we no longer have to choose between being vegan and eating the foods that feed our hearts, minds, and traditions as well as our bodies.

My family, my friends, and my puppy love gravy—biscuits and gravy, mashed potatoes and gravy, holiday vegan roast and gravy, and even V-Dog and gravy. Salads need a creamy or tangy dressing, and biscuits need jam. And vegan cheese sauce means your vegetables (and you) need never be cheese deprived. The following recipes have you covered from January to December. Keep your vegan umami essentials like tamari, nutritional yeast, capers, miso, and mushrooms close by and get ready to revive some of your favorite meals.

Ultimate Marinade

Picture this: You're whipping up some marinade for a family cook-out and someone says, "Hey, your marinade smells so wonderful I could drink it straight." What? Like a shot of Maker's Mark? You might think that's weird, or you could just pull out a red Solo cup and invite your guest to belly up to the kitchen counter. Either way, it's a compliment that should make you feel darn good about your marinade. This recipe is a version of the one my family has used for grilling as far back as I can remember. I have amped up the flavor with some minced garlic and red wine vinegar. It can be used for grilling burgers, kebabs, or veggies or brushed on seitan, tempeh, or tofu to deliver a denser flavor.

¼ cup extra virgin olive oil

¼ cup tamari

2 tablespoons vegan
Worcestershire sauce

2 tablespoons red wine
vinegar

1 tablespoon minced garlic

Combine all the ingredients in a small mixing bowl and whisk until thoroughly combined. This marinade can be stored in the refrigerator for 2–3 days.

Serves 8.

Smoky Barbecue Sauce

Not long after I graduated from pharmacy school, I took a job with a company based in Richmond, Virginia. My workspace was in Kentucky, but I frequently traveled to Virginia to meet with my boss Pam, who happened to be a transplant from New York. During these meetings, she made every effort to be a gracious hostess to those of us from other states, although she seemed to be mystified by the food and culture of her new southern home. During one visit, she announced we would be going out for something called BBQ and then launched into a lengthy lecture on what BBQ is, describing it as small bits of cooked meat with a spicy sauce. She went on to say that she really didn't understand what all the fuss was about, but since Virginians seemed so proud of their BBQ, we should probably give it a try. I assured her that Kentuckians were familiar with BBQ, so she needn't tax herself with further explanation. She seemed genuinely surprised that this strange fare had breached state boundaries. I can only imagine the conversation when my North Carolina counterpart visited.

My favorite barbecue sauce has evolved over the years, with the addition of chipotle in adobo being the most recent variation. It has a deep, smoky, slightly sweet flavor with plenty of spice. I use it for barbecue seitan sandwiches, grilled chick'n, slow-cooked seitan, cheese grits, or vegan pork-flavored bites.

2 tablespoons extra virgin olive oil
1 medium onion, chopped
1 tablespoon minced garlic
½ cup vegan India pale ale (IPA)
1 chipotle in adobo
¼ cup sorghum syrup
½ cup tomato paste
1 tablespoon tamari
1 teaspoon cumin
1 teaspoon smoked paprika
1 teaspoon vegan Worcestershire sauce
1 teaspoon Dijon mustard
3 tablespoons apple cider vinegar
½ cup water
Dash liquid smoke

Heat the olive oil in a saucepan over medium-high heat. Add the onion and garlic and cook for 10 minutes, or until the onions are translucent. Add the IPA, bring to a simmer, and cook for 5 minutes. Add the remaining ingredients and simmer for 30 minutes. Incorporate into recipes as needed. This sauce keeps for 5 days in the refrigerator.

Serves 8.

Sawmill Gravy

To say we like gravy in Kentucky is an understatement. Every Sunday morning we would loll about the living room waiting for my stepmom, Jo—prone to lots of talking and very slow cooking—to bring the gravy to the table. And nothing makes biscuits or country fried steak happier than this flavorful vegan sausage gravy. It is simple to make, requires minimal ingredients, and is virtually foolproof. This recipe is so close to traditional gravy that my former spouse's family has adopted it as their holiday gravy, even though none of them are vegan or even vegetarian. I like to use Gimme Lean sausage and unsweetened oat or soy milk for this recipe, but any ground vegan sausage and plant-based milk will do. Combine it with a hearty breakfast or let your biscuits and gravy fly solo with a side of fruit.

12 ounces ground plant-based sausage
2 tablespoons olive oil
2 tablespoons vegan butter
¼ cup unbleached all-purpose flour

1 teaspoon sea salt
1 teaspoon freshly ground black pepper
2½ cups unsweetened oat milk

Heat the olive oil and butter in a skillet over medium-high heat, add the sausage, and cook for 5–7 minutes, until nicely browned. Use a fork to break up any large pieces of sausage. Sprinkle the flour, salt, and pepper over the sausage and continue cooking and stirring for another 3 minutes. Pour the milk into the skillet and stir until the gravy is thick and bubbly. If you prefer a thinner gravy, add a bit more milk and heat through. Remove from the heat and serve immediately.

Serves 4.

Thanksgiving Gravy

The scent of this gravy conjures up all things holiday. The thyme and sage combine with the toasted nutritional yeast to make a delicious topping for mashed potatoes and the centerpiece of your holiday table, whether it's the popularly spoofed Tofurky or your own vegan roast. It keeps for a couple of days covered and refrigerated, so you can make it ahead of time and cross it off the holiday prep list. And don't think you have to reserve it for special occasions. It's relatively simple to make, so if you're yearning for some mashed potatoes and gravy, get to work.

½ cup nutritional yeast
½ cup unbleached all-purpose
    flour
⅓ cup canola oil
2 large shallots, finely
    chopped
1 tablespoon minced garlic
2 teaspoons dried thyme

1 teaspoon ground sage
2 cups water
1 cup dry white wine
1 cup no-chicken broth
¼ cup tamari
¾ teaspoon sea salt
1 teaspoon freshly ground
    black pepper

Whisk together the nutritional yeast and flour until well combined. Stir over medium heat in a heavy skillet for 5–7 minutes, until lightly toasted. Set aside to cool. In a heavy medium-sized saucepan, heat the canola oil over medium-low heat and add the shallots, garlic, thyme, and sage. Cook, stirring constantly, for 5 minutes, or until the mixture is fragrant and the shallots are translucent, being careful not to overbrown the garlic. Whisk in the flour mixture and stir until well combined. Add the water, wine, broth, tamari, salt, and pepper; turn the heat up to medium; and whisk until all the ingredients are fully incorporated. Bring to a simmer and continue to cook, stirring frequently, until the gravy thickens. Use a mesh strainer to pour the gravy into a bowl. Serve immediately or store covered and refrigerated for up to 2 days. Reheat prior to serving.

Serves 8–10.

Mushroom Gravy

I usually use this gravy for seitan sandwiches (see chapter 3).
However, if you are a mushroom lover like me, it is equally good
over vegan steak or any time you are serving mashed potatoes
as a side dish. I love the subtle flavor of the shallots and fresh
parsley. White mushrooms are listed because they are available
almost everywhere year-round, but feel free to substitute your
mushroom of choice.

2 tablespoons extra virgin
    olive oil
1 extra large shallot, finely
    chopped
1 teaspoon minced garlic
8 ounces white mushrooms,
    thinly sliced
2 cups vegetable broth
2 tablespoons tamari

½ teaspoon dried thyme
2 tablespoons chopped fresh
    parsley
½ teaspoon sea salt
½ teaspoon freshly ground
    black pepper
2 tablespoons cornstarch
¼ cup water

Heat the olive oil in a saucepan over medium heat. Add the shallot
and cook for 5 minutes, until soft. Add the garlic and mushrooms
and cook for 2 minutes. Stir in the broth, tamari, thyme, parsley,
salt, and pepper and bring to a boil. Reduce the heat and simmer
for 5 minutes. Blend the cornstarch and water and stir into the
mushroom mixture. Cook over low heat for 5–10 minutes. Serve
immediately or cover and refrigerate for 2–3 days.

Serves 8.

Ranch Dressing and Dip

This recipe may seem like an anomaly with its powdered herbs
and crushed saltines, but it's for those people who come to my
home demanding great vats of ranch dressing (they know who
they are). Somehow, ranch dressing has become as American as
apple pie. It's put on everything from sandwiches to pizza. I'm

pretty sure my nephews Patrick and Lennon came into the world with tiny ranch mustaches. I've had this recipe jotted down on a notepad for so long I can't even remember its origin. The important thing is, when the hard-core ranchers show up, I'm prepared.

DRY MIX

15 saltines
2 cups parsley flakes
½ cup dried minced onion
2 tablespoons dill weed

¼ cup onion salt
¼ cup onion powder
¼ cup garlic salt
¼ cup garlic powder

DRESSING OR DIP

2 teaspoons apple cider
   vinegar
1 cup unsweetened soy milk
¼ teaspoon cayenne

¾ cup vegan mayonnaise
¼ cup vegan sour cream (for
   dressing) or 10 ounces
   vegan sour cream (for dip)

Place all the ingredients for the dry mix in a food processor and pulse until well combined. To mix the dressing, add the vinegar to the almond milk and set aside for a few minutes to thicken. Add cayenne and 1½ tablespoons dry mix to vegan mayo and ¼ cup vegan sour cream. Combine with the milk mixture and chill for 2 hours before serving. To mix the dip, stir 2 tablespoons dry mix into 10 ounces vegan sour cream and mix well. Chill for 2 hours or overnight to let the flavors meld.

Serves 8–10.

Tomato Vinaigrette

Kentucky summers provide an abundance of fresh basil and tomatoes. This simple salad dressing makes good use of both and adds an unequaled layer of freshness to tossed greens or pasta salad. It's also easy to throw together at the last minute if you happen to make some weird, impromptu creation that didn't turn out as planned. (I'm not speaking from personal experience, of course.)

1½ cups good-quality olive oil

1 large ripe tomato, chopped with juice

1 bunch fresh basil, chopped

¼ cup chopped fresh parsley

¼ cup sherry vinegar

1 clove garlic, chopped

2 teaspoons sorghum syrup

1 teaspoon sea salt

1 teaspoon freshly ground black pepper

Place all the ingredients in a blender or food processor and process until smooth. Chill until ready to serve.

Serves 8.

Basic Vegan Cheese Sauce

This sauce is the foundation for several recipes. I modify it with various seasonings and spices, depending on how I intend to use it. I serve this sauce at least once a week with steamed broccoli or cauliflower, as well as variations of it for mac and cheese, tacos, or nachos. If you have a high-powered blender, soaking the cashews is optional, but I think soaking results in a superior creamy texture.

½ cup whole raw cashews, soaked in filtered water for 8 hours

½ cup water

1 cup no-chicken broth

1 7-ounce block vegan cheddar, chopped

1 teaspoon mellow white miso (optional)

½ stick vegan butter

¼ cup unbleached all-purpose flour

Drain and rinse the cashews and place in the blender with the water and broth. Process for 2–3 minutes, until completely smooth. Add the remaining ingredients and process on soup speed for an additional 3 minutes.

Makes approximately 3 cups.

Red Wine Dijon Vinaigrette

I love a tangy vinaigrette with some fresh salad greens. Summer harvests just wouldn't be the same without this dressing. It's also my favorite for pasta salad, any mixed vegetable salad, and fresh steamed asparagus.

1 cup good-quality olive oil
1–2 teaspoons chopped garlic
¼ cup red wine vinegar
1 tablespoon Dijon mustard
1 teaspoon freshly ground
    black pepper

½ teaspoon sea salt
2 tablespoons Italian
    seasoning
Juice of 2 medium lemons
1 tablespoon tamari

Combine all the ingredients in a bowl and whisk well. Taste and adjust seasoning.

Serves 8–10.

Maple Butter

Be warned that this sweet, creamy vegan butter is addictive. I make it as a special treat for the holidays, and it's delicious with biscuits, pancakes, or waffles. It keeps well for at least 10 days. This is the only item my coworker Lisa insists we include on the employee party menu, and any leftovers go home with her.

1 cup pure maple syrup
2-inch cinnamon stick

1½ sticks vegan butter

In a medium saucepan, bring the maple syrup and cinnamon stick to a boil over medium-high heat. Cook for 15 minutes, stirring to prevent sticking. Remove the pan from the heat, discard the cinnamon stick, and stir in the vegan butter until melted. Transfer the mixture to the bowl of an electric mixer. Use the paddle attachment to beat until the mixture is creamy and opaque, around 7–8 minutes.

Serves 8–10.

Brown Sauce/Gravy

This rich, tasty sauce complements a multitude of dishes. The herbs and tamari give it depth of flavor, and the vegan sour cream amps up the creamy texture. I serve it over country fried steak or mashed potatoes. If you have leftovers, add them to soup or stew.

3 tablespoons vegan butter
1 small yellow onion, finely chopped
½ cup finely chopped carrots
½ cup finely chopped celery
1 tablespoon minced garlic
1 bay leaf
¼ cup unbleached all-purpose flour
2 cups vegetable broth, divided

1 vegan beef bouillon cube
¼ cup dry red wine
2 tablespoons tamari
½ teaspoon dried thyme
½ teaspoon dried parsley
1 teaspoon onion powder
1 tablespoon vegan sour cream
Salt and freshly ground black pepper

Heat the vegan butter over medium heat. Add the onion, carrots, celery, garlic, and bay leaf and cook until the vegetables soften and the onion is translucent. Sprinkle the flour over the vegetable mixture, stir until completely combined, and cook for 5 minutes. Add 1 cup broth and the bouillon cube. Cook, stirring constantly, until the mixture is thick and bubbly. Add the remaining 1 cup broth, wine, tamari, thyme, parsley, and onion powder. Cook, stirring as needed, for an additional 20 minutes. Remove from the heat and strain through a sieve to remove the vegetables and bay leaf. Stir in the vegan sour cream. Season with salt and pepper to taste. Serve hot.

Serves 6–8.

Tartar Sauce

Capers are the vegan's ally. Neither a fruit nor a vegetable, they are the immature flower buds of a plant that grows abundantly in the Mediterranean. When pickled, they pack a delicious combination of salt and acid that amps up a dish's flavor profile—it's like the Godzilla of vegan umami has paid you a visit. This simple sauce is ideal for any faux fish dish, but it's also great on a burger with some shredded lettuce and vegan cheese.

½ cup vegan mayonnaise

¼ cup capers

1 tablespoon finely chopped
  fresh parsley

1 teaspoon minced shallot

1 tablespoon Dijon mustard

1 tablespoon white wine
  vinegar

¼ teaspoon dried dill

Sea salt and freshly ground
  black pepper to taste

Dash Tabasco

Combine all the ingredients in a blender or food processor and process until smooth. Chill until ready to serve.

Serves 8.

Toasted Pumpkin Seed Dressing

Bibb lettuce right from the garden was a regular feature of my family's summertime dinner table. My grandparents liked to top their garden bounty with some hot bacon grease for what was known as a wilted greens salad. Even as a nonvegan eight-year-old, I recoiled at this travesty. Who wanted a wilted salad with grease on it? The obvious answer was my grandfather, who laughed at my wrinkled-up nose, tossed some scallions on top, and chomped away like a cow in clover. Though I never learned to embrace that particular iteration of a salad, I do love this dressing, which has a smoky bacon-like flavor and is ideal for simple garden greens. Serve warm or at room temperature, and if you like, throw in a few sunflower seeds and scallions for texture.

½ cup raw pumpkin seeds
1 shallot, chopped
½ cup good-quality olive oil
6 tablespoons red wine
   vinegar
2 tablespoons nutritional
   yeast

1 teaspoon liquid smoke
1 teaspoon red pepper flakes
1 teaspoon sea salt
2 tablespoons sorghum syrup
1 tablespoon water

Preheat oven to 400 degrees. Place a single layer of pumpkins seeds on a baking sheet and toast for 5–10 minutes, or until golden brown. Oven temperatures vary, so keep a close eye on them to avoid overbrowning. Set aside to cool. Sauté the shallot in the olive oil for 5 minutes and set aside to cool. Once the ingredients have reached room temperature, add the pumpkins seeds, the shallot, and the remaining ingredients to a blender and process until relatively smooth. Don't worry if a few pumpkin seeds remain intact. This just adds to the texture and visual appeal.

Serves 8–10.

Hazel's Cranberry Sauce

Although a poll is unlikely to find many people who claim cranberry sauce as their favorite dish, we're not willing to forgo it on the holiday table. There's the canned gelatinous version, of course, but this one will steal the show. My sons' aunt Hazel, a phenomenal cook and baker, always brought this dish to Thanksgiving dinner. I was quick to ask for the recipe, and it has remained in the canon ever since. Its unusual combination of flavors hits all the right notes and is a perfect counter to rich foods. When cranberries are in season, try it with a vegetable plate or a vegan pot roast with fluffy rolls.

2 cups whole cranberries   ½ cup sugar

1 small onion   2 tablespoons horseradish

¾ cup vegan sour cream

Place the cranberries in a food processor and pulse until broken up but still chunky. Mix with the remaining ingredients and store in the refrigerator until ready to serve. It can also be prepared ahead and frozen for up to 1 week. Just thaw it in the refrigerator for several hours prior to serving.

Serves 8–10.

Strawberry Freezer Jam

I remember jars of this brightly colored staple stored in the freezer, ready to thaw and spread on biscuits on Sunday mornings. My niece Autumn reminded me just how delicious it is when she brought two jars on a recent visit. My household was smitten. For several days, any bread served was accompanied by the phrase, "You know what would be good on this?" Concerned that our two jars wouldn't last long, I feverishly jotted down the recipe. However, Autumn's six-year-old expressed the most worry, questioning his mother about the adequacy of their at-home jam inventory. Autumn reassured him that they had twenty jars in the pantry. I have a feeling he's staked out there, protecting their jam supply with a Nerf gun. You'll understand once you make a batch.

1 pound fresh strawberries   1 1.75-ounce box fruit pectin

4 cups sugar   ¾ cup water

Pulse the berries in a food processor until chopped but still chunky. Add sugar to the berries and mix well. Let sit at room temperature for 10 minutes. Mix the fruit pectin and water in a saucepan and bring to a boil. Boil over high heat for 1 minute. Pour the liquid over the berries and let sit for 3 minutes, or until the sugar is completely dissolved. Ladle into canning jars, leaving

½ inch space at the top. Cover with lids. Let the jars stand at room temperature for 24 hours. Store tightly sealed in the refrigerator for 3 weeks or freeze for up to 1 year.

Makes 6 cups.

About the Author

Jan A. Brandenburg is a cook, digital content creator, yoga instructor, and pharmacist from eastern Kentucky. Wanting to enjoy the flavors of her childhood while supporting her values and love for animals, she has spent years developing plant-based alternatives to traditional Appalachian dishes. She lives, works, and teaches in Berea, Kentucky. Find her on Instagram @appalachianvegan.

Blue Eye Views/Miranda Dowdy

Index